HOLINESS OF
HEART AND LIFE

HOLINESS OF HEART AND LIFE

Stephen A. Seamands

ABINGDON PRESS
Nashville

HOLINESS OF HEART AND LIFE

Copyright © 1990 by Abingdon Press

This book is printed on acid-free paper.

Library of Congress Cataloging-in-Publication Data

SEAMANDS, STEPHEN A., 1949–
    Holiness of heart and life / Stephen A. Seamands.
        p.   cm.—(Faithful congregations series)
    ISBN 0-687-12652-5 (alk. paper)
    1. Spiritual life—Methodist authors. 2. Church renewal—United Methodist Church (U.S.) 3. United Methodist Church (U.S.)—Doctrines. 4. Methodist Church—Doctrines. 5. Holiness—Christianity.   I. Title.   II. Series.
BX8349.H64S42   1990
248.4′876—dc20   90-23253
                                                                        CIP

Scripture quotations unless otherwise noted are from The Holy Bible, New Revised Standard Version, *copyright © 1989 by the Division of Christian Education of the National Council of the Churches of Christ in the United States of America. All emphases are the author's.*

Quotations marked KJV are from the King James Version of the Bible.

MANUFACTURED IN THE UNITED STATES OF AMERICA

To my grandfather, **E. A. Seamands** *(1891–1984)*
Engineer, Evangelist, Missionary to India
Whose life so clearly reflected the beauty of holiness

Contents

Introduction

"Do you think you could take me over to Vineland to the site of the historic camp meeting?" my eighty-nine-year-old grandfather asked. He had come from his home in Kentucky to visit our family in southern New Jersey where I was serving as a United Methodist pastor. In examining a map before he came, he had observed that we lived only ten miles from Vineland. So he wanted to make sure he got there while he was with us.

Camp meetings had played an important part in my grandfather's life. He had been converted at a camp meeting in August, 1912. At that same camp meeting God had dramatically called him to serve as a missionary to India. In 1923, four years after he arrived in India, he and another missionary initiated the annual Dharhur Jatre, an indigenous version of the camp meeting adapted from the Hindu Jatra (religious festival). Today this annual event is attended by more than one hundred thousand Christians and serves as a well-spring for spiritual renewal within the South India Annual Conference of The United Methodist Church.

Because camp meetings were so significant in his own life

and ministry, he became an avid reader of the history of the camp meeting movement in the United States. That's how he knew about Vineland. In 1867 a camp meeting was held there which opened a new chapter in the history of the American camp meeting. What was unique about the camp meeting at Vineland was its emphasis on holiness. Camp meetings had thrived in America for more than fifty years; but generally they focused on the conversion of sinners, not the holiness of believers.

However, beginning in the 1830s there was a revived interest among American Methodists in holiness of heart and life, and particularly the early Methodist emphasis on the experience of Christian perfection or entire sanctification. As a result, a group of prominent Methodist pastors from Philadelphia, New York, Baltimore, as well as several other cities in Pennsylvania and New Jersey, met together in June, 1867. Following their meeting, they issued a call to anyone, regardless of denomination, who wished to join them on July 17 at Vineland, New Jersey, for a camp meeting that would focus especially on holiness.

The response far exceeded their expectations. Church historian Melvin Dieter describes what happened at Vineland:

> Crowded trains stopped at the Cape May Railroad station; long lines of buggies thronged the roads which led to the forty acre public park on the edge of town which served as the campsite. Overnight the town's population swelled to almost double its 10,000 regular inhabitants as hundreds of tents sprang up around the speaker's stand on the campground. For ten days the campers listened to sermons and exhortations on the theme of Christian holiness by members of the organizing committee and Bishop Matthew Simpson.[1]

This incredible response was generated by the passion for holiness of heart and life among the Methodists of that time. They were convinced that this was the primary reason God had raised them up: to spread scriptural holiness across the land. And they did not want their church to lose sight of that. At the close of the Vineland camp a decision was made to create an organization—the National Camp Meeting Association for the Promotion of Holiness. Over the next twenty-five years that organization was at the forefront of the renewed emphasis on holiness within Methodism and many other denominations. The camp where my grandfather was converted, and hundreds of others like it, was an outgrowth of what began at Vineland.

So my grandfather wanted me to take him to the site of the historic camp meeting.

"I'm not exactly sure where it's located," I said to him. "I think it's at a park in the northern part of town. But let's go. We'll drive around until we find it."

Half an hour later we arrived at the park and began to look around for the marker that was supposed to be there. It was the middle of the day. Children were still in school. No one was playing. We were the only ones there. No voices were to be heard, only the wind blowing in the trees and causing the swings to clang against their metal framework.

We looked and looked for the marker, but couldn't find it. "It's got to be here somewhere," I assured my grandfather. "Look at the grove of trees. It's a perfect place for a camp meeting." But everything we approached which we thought might be a marker turned out to be something else.

After we had searched for a long time and were almost ready to give up, we came across a large rock about three feet tall in the midst of several evergreen bushes. There we found what we were looking for. A plaque had been inlaid on the rock. The words on the plaque indicated that this was the site of the historic camp meeting held in August, 1867.

"So this is it," my grandfather said as his eyes scanned the park.

"This is it," I replied. And suddenly I found myself struck

by the great contrast between the way that place must have looked during that camp meeting and the way it looked now. I imagined the huge crowd of people gathered on that site. I visualized the rows of tents across the grounds. I could hear the people's spirited singing. I could picture them listening intently to the preachers and responding in large numbers to their invitations. Above all, I sensed the passion for holiness that had caused such a great throng of people to assemble in the first place.

Something momentous had happened in that very spot. But in looking at the park now—empty, quiet, somewhat rundown—who would ever know it? There was nothing left to show for it all—only an obscure marker which hardly anyone knew existed.

We walked around the park a bit more. Then we went back to the car and headed for home. But on the way back, I began to think about the church I love—The United Methodist Church. Holiness of heart and life—that was once our great passion. That passion caused Methodist churches to spring up all across the American frontier. That passion drew people to the camp meeting at Vineland. But what about now? Where is our passion for holiness today? Like the park which was the site of that camp meeting, does anyone even know what we once were? Does anyone today associate Methodism with holiness?

This book is written with the hope that United Methodist congregations might recover that passion for holiness of heart and life which once characterized the Methodist movement. The risen Christ said to the church at Ephesus, "I have this against you, that you have abandoned the love you had at first. Remember then from what you have fallen; repent, and do the works you did at first" (Rev. 2:4-5). Like the Ephesians, we Methodists have lost our first love—our passion for holiness. But there can be a renewal of holiness in our midst. Like the Ephesians, if we repent and do what we did at first, holiness can again become our first love.

May what is presented in these pages help start recovering that passion. Then God will raise up a new people called Methodists—a people, like the early Methodists, with a passion for holiness.

Note

1. Melvin E. Dieter, *The Holiness Revival of the Nineteenth Century* (Metuchen, N.J.: The Scarecrow Press, 1980), p. 106.

1

The Lost Treasure of Methodism

If you were to ask twenty-five United Methodist church leaders to describe the purpose and mission of United Methodism as it stands on the threshold of the twenty-first century, you would likely get twenty-five widely divergent answers. It is no secret: we are a denomination that lacks a clear consensus of who we are and what we are supposed to be doing. Although we are involved in a wide range of worthwhile concerns and activities, a disjointedness about our church life exists at every level. We are like a bicycle wheel that has many spokes but no hub. We lack a unifying center, something that binds all we do together and is connected to a source of power which can move us forward.

In marked contrast to contemporary United Methodism, John Wesley and the early Methodists had a clear sense of identity and mission. Whenever he was asked what Methodism was and why God had raised it up, Wesley's answer always revolved around one thing: holiness of heart and life. Consider these representative statements:

> The essence of it [Methodism] is holiness of heart and life; the circumstantials all point to this.[1]

By Methodists I mean a people who profess to pursue (in whatsoever measure they have attained) holiness of heart and life, inward and outward conformity in all things to the revealed will of God.[2]

We [the Methodists] set out upon two principles: (1) None go to heaven without holiness of heart and life; (2) whoever follows after this (whatever his opinions be) is my 'brother and sister and mother.' And we have not swerved an hair's breadth from either one or the other of these to this day.[3]

Q.3 What may we reasonably believe to be God's design in raising up the Preachers called Methodists?
A. Not to form any new sect; but to reform the nation, particularly the Church; and to spread scriptural holiness over the land.
Q.4 What was the rise of Methodism, so called?
A. In 1729, two young men, reading the Bible, saw they could not be saved without holiness, followed after it, and incited others so to do. In 1737 they saw holiness comes by faith. They saw likewise, that men are justified before they are sanctified; but still holiness was their point. God then thrust them out, utterly against their will, to raise a holy people.[4]

Wesley and the early Methodists were sure about their identity and mission. Methodism had been raised up to promote holiness in every sphere of life—in the individual, the church, society and the world. Holiness was the hub of the wheel which held all the spokes together. Holiness was the burning focus, the driving force of the movement. Spreading scriptural holiness was early Methodism's magnificent obsession and paramount goal. Once this is understood, all the major emphases in Wesley's theology and practice begin to fall into place. His emphases upon prevenient grace, evangelism and the new birth, the means of grace, personal ethics, societies and class meetings, social justice, and Christian perfection all flow from his passion for holiness.

Later this same passion motivated the early Methodists in America and was largely responsible for the remarkable growth of Methodism in the United States, particularly in the first half of the nineteenth century. In his address at the Methodist centenary celebration in 1866, John McClintock, first president of Drew Seminary, underscored the importance of this emphasis on holiness and urged Methodism not to depart from it:

> Knowing exactly what I say, and taking the full responsibility of it, I repeat, we are the only church in history, from the apostles' time until now, that has put forward as its very elemental thought—the great central pervading idea of the whole book of God from the beginning to the end—the holiness of the human soul, heart, mind, and will. . . . Our work is a moral work—that is to say, the work of making men holy. Our preaching is for that, our church agencies are for that, our schools, colleges, universities, and theological seminaries are for that. There is our mission—there is our glory—there is our power, and there shall be the ground of our triumph. God keep us true.[5]

However as time went on Methodism, by-and-large, drifted away from its original purpose and mission. By the beginning of the twentieth century, its passion for holiness had waned and was being supplanted by other interests. In a 1974 address, Albert Outler acknowledged this decline of interest in holiness and lamented its consequences:

> The doctrine of holiness of heart and life that had been the keystone in the arch of Wesley's doctrine, by the turn of this century had become a pebble in the shoe of standard bred Methodists. And presently they took off the shoe, threw out the pebble, put the shoe back on and kept walking, with the same labels but without the same equipment. And this has been an uncomprehended and immense tragedy for all who claim John Wesley as their father in God.[6]

As a result the majority of United Methodists today have little or no awareness of our original purpose and mission. Holiness of heart and life has become the lost treasure of Methodism.

The Path to Recovery

But how do we recover a passion for holiness? A few years ago, I would have urged a recovery and restatement of Wesley's understanding of holiness. I had even begun to write a book with that in mind. Now, however, as much as I appreciate Wesley and applaud the attempts being made to call our church back to his theology, I am no longer convinced that is the path we should take.

We desperately need to catch a fresh vision of holiness and to be infused with the same passion for holiness which inspired Wesley and the early Methodists. But the way to create that vision and passion in our congregations is not by looking primarily to Wesley. In the eighteenth century, Wesley's presentation of the call to holiness spoke profoundly to the people and was extremely effective in spreading scriptural holiness. But that was two hundred fifty years ago. And although the call to holiness has not changed, the way that call is presented must change if it is going to speak to the needs of people in our day.

As wonderful and as precious as it was, the way Wesley presented holiness is now an old wineskin. Put new wine into it and it will burst. Trying to restore our passion for holiness by patching the old wineskin or trying to modify it simply will not do. We need a new wineskin to contain the new wine of holiness that God wants to pour out upon us today.

But if a reappropriation and restatement of Wesley isn't the answer, to what should we turn? We must turn to the source Christians seek when they need fresh vision and inspiration. We must turn to the Bible. As we reflect and meditate upon the Scriptures, the written word of God, through the work of the Holy Spirit we are brought face to face with the living Word, Jesus Christ. Only out of an encounter with him will come the new vision and passion for holiness needed today.

Of course, this does not mean that we ought to abandon

Wesley altogether. He had many helpful and abiding insights into scriptural holiness which we can appropriate today. Later we will discuss some of his insights. We will also use major events in Wesley's life story as we present the necessary ingredients for rekindling a passion for holiness. Nevertheless, Wesley is of secondary value to us. He is useful only when he serves as a pointer beyond himself to our primary source—Scripture itself, which in turn points beyond itself to the living Christ.

The truth is most United Methodist congregations are so far removed from the vision of holiness which inspired Wesley and the early Methodists that they are not sure what holiness of heart and life is. *Holiness*—the very word itself has lost any real meaning and power for most United Methodists. For some it is primarily a negative word—that leaves a bad taste in their mouths. It evokes images of dour, somber Christians. "God's frozen chosen," as they have been called, measure the depth of their spirituality by the depth of their misery. They deny the basic goodness of human life, retreat into spiritual ghettos and shun active involvement in the world.

For others holiness has no negative connotations, but it evokes nothing positive either—no sense of the beauty of holiness or its compelling, attractive power. For many it has become a bland, meaningless term.

So we need to get back to basics, back to the Scriptures to discover again what holiness is and to receive a new vision and fresh passion for holiness of heart and life.

Letting Isaiah Speak to Us

Since holiness is one of the grand themes of the Bible, we could cite many different passages in seeking to recover an understanding of holiness of heart and life for today. We will, however, focus our attention on Isaiah 6:1-8 and examine that passage in detail, with the hope that it can serve as a window through which we can catch a vision of the biblical understanding of holiness.

In Isaiah 6:1-8 we find the familiar account of Isaiah's vision of God, along with his call and commissioning as a prophet. Above all, the holiness of God confronts Isaiah. "Holy, holy, holy"—the cry of the seraphs, the heavenly beings Isaiah saw hovering around the throne of God—captures the essence of his vision. Holiness is a central motif throughout the entire book of Isaiah. Isaiah's favorite title for God, "the Holy One of Israel," is found twenty-six times throughout the book. Thus Isaiah 6:1-8 is an appropriate passage for us to consider.

However, before we turn directly to Isaiah's vision, we need to examine the five chapters which precede it. These chapters set the stage and create the context for the prophet's vision. In Isaiah 1–5 we are given a description of Israel, the people of God, during the days of Isaiah the prophet. It is a picture of a people which has completely and deliberately turned its back upon God.

At the very outset, Isaiah identifies their basic problem: "I reared children and brought them up, but they have rebelled against me. . . . Ah, sinful nation, people laden with iniquity, offspring who do evil, children who deal corruptly, who have forsaken the Lord, who have despised the Holy One of Israel, who are utterly estranged" (1:2,4). Then the prophet spells out in vivid detail the specific sins of the people which have flowed out of their fundamental rebellion against God. They have become proud and haughty. They have exalted themselves in the place of God (2:11, 17; 3:16; 5:21). They worship the creation rather than the Creator. They bow down to idols they have made (2:8). They care only about accumulating wealth and increasing military power (2:7; 3:18-23; 5:8). They are caught up in the relentless pursuit of personal pleasure (5:11-12, 22). They oppress the weak and the helpless (5:23). They "grind the face of the poor" (3:15). They have lost the capacity for moral discernment. They confuse evil with good and good with evil (5:20).

In chapter 5 Isaiah brings his description of the people to a climax with a love song, a song about an unfruitful vineyard: "My beloved had a vineyard on a very fertile hill. He dug it and cleared it of stones, and planted it with choice vines; he built a watchtower in the midst of it, and hewed out a wine vat in it; he expected it to yield grapes, but it yielded wild grapes" (vv. 1-2).

God did everything he possibly could for his people. But the people did not respond to God's goodness. Instead of producing fruits of holiness, they became unholy and unrighteous and unclean. Now they stand under God's judgment:

> I will tell you what I will do to my vineyard. I will remove its hedge, and it shall be devoured; I will break down its wall, and it shall be trampled down. I will make it a waste; it shall not be pruned or hoed, and it shall be overgrown with briers and thorns; I will also command the clouds that they rain no rain upon it. (vv. 5-6)

Yet in the midst of these five chapters detailing Israel's sins and God's judgment, there are two brief passages where we are given a completely different picture of God's people (2:1-4; 4:2-6). In these verses we get a glimpse of a people restored and redeemed, a holy people among whom righteousness and peace prevail, a people who dwell in the presence of God and who order their lives according to his will.

And so in the first five chapters of Isaiah, the prophet also holds out the striking possibility of a radical transformation: an unholy people (arrogant, unrighteous, self-centered) can become a holy people (humble, righteous, serving).

But the question naturally arises: how can such an

incredible transformation take place? No explicit answer to that question is given. However, it would seem that Isaiah's experience in chapter 6, by its very placement after the first five chapters, is meant to provide the answer. Here we have a description of one person's encounter with God. If what was experienced by that one person could be expanded to the whole people of God, restoration and renewal would result. If what happened to Isaiah also happened to others, an unholy people would become a holy people. Isaiah's experience contains all the necessary ingredients for the renewal of our congregations. So let's see what happened to him.

Notes

1. *The Works of John Wesley*, vol. 13 (Grand Rapids: Zondervan Publishing House, 1958), p. 260 (hereafter cited as *Works*).
2. *Works*, 8, p. 352.
3. *The Letters of John Wesley*, ed. John Telford, vol. 6 (London: Epworth Press, 1931), p. 61 (hereafter cited as *Letters*).
4. *Works*, 8, pp. 299-300.
5. Quoted in Olin A. Curtis, *The Christian Faith* (New York: Eaton and Mains, 1905), p. 372.
6. Albert Outler, "Whither Wesleyan Theology," a lecture given at Asbury Theological Seminary, March 14, 1974.

2

If My People
Will Humble
Themselves . . .

"In the year that King Uzziah died, I saw the Lord." So
Isaiah begins his account of his vision of God. And at first
glance it would appear that there is nothing particularly
important here—just an attempt to establish the date when
his vision occurred. Yet in these seemingly insignificant
words, Isaiah is putting his finger on one of the key
ingredients necessary for the transformation of an unholy
people to a holy people. It is a prerequisite for all that follows.
That ingredient—brokenness, humility, poverty of spirit—is
what we want to think about in this chapter.

The Death of a King

"In the year that *King Uzziah* died." Who was King Uzziah,
anyway? In II Chronicles 26 we are given a detailed account
of his reign. We learn that he was sixteen years old when he
was crowned king of Judah, and he reigned for a long
time—fifty-two years!

But Uzziah's reign was not only long, it was also grand and majestic. Uzziah was the greatest king since Solomon. Not since the Queen of Sheba had knelt at Solomon's feet had the national pride been so high or the nation's sovereignty extended to such remote borders. This renowned king had two names: Uzziah, which means "Yahweh his strength," and Azariah (II Kings 14:21), which means "Yahweh his helper." And truly God had been his help and his strength. The chronicler tells us "his fame spread far, for he was marvelously helped until he became strong" (II Chron. 26:15). Uzziah took the kingdom of Judah to dazzling heights of prosperity and glory. He was a victorious general and a brilliant administrator.

Think of how his glory must have affected young Isaiah. Isaiah had never known any other king. Uzziah was his hero and his idol. Like every other youth in the kingdom, Isaiah felt that Uzziah not only sat upon the throne of the palace, but also on the throne of Isaiah's heart. Isaiah's hopes and dreams for the nation and for his own life were wrapped up in the power and glory of this stately king.

But unfortunately Uzziah's reign, which had begun in faithfulness and obedience to God, ended in shame and humiliation. The Scripture says that when Uzziah "had become strong he grew proud, to his destruction" (II Chron. 26:16). In his conceited arrogance, he thought he could take the place of the priests. He thought he could dispense with God's appointed order and do things any way he pleased. Why not? Wasn't he the king?

So one day he entered the temple and went into the holy place where only a priest was allowed to go. He, not the priest, would offer his sacrifice to the Lord. But when he came out, he was no longer a proud and glorious king. Instead Uzziah staggered out a leper, broken, humiliated, and worst of all unclean "because the Lord had struck him" (v. 20). From that time on Uzziah was forced to move out of the palace and live according to the strict laws governing lepers. Although he was the king of Israel—the greatest since Solomon—he became an outcast living in a place of quarantine and separation.

Can you imagine the impact this must have had on young Isaiah? His great king, his hero, his ideal—a leper! But surely it would not last. Surely God would heal him and restore him to his throne. No. The chronicler says, "King Uzziah was leprous to the day of his death, and being leprous lived in a separate house, for he was excluded from the house of the Lord" (v. 21).

What a blow this must have been to Isaiah! Uzziah, the mightiest monarch of the times, Uzziah dead—and dead as a leper! The one on whom he had pinned his hopes and dreams had died in disgrace. Not only then was the throne of Israel emptied when Uzziah died, the throne of Isaiah's heart was emptied too.

Yet this emptying was absolutely essential. It was necessary if Isaiah were to see God. His own throne had to be emptied before he could see God "sitting on a throne." His false gods had to be brought low before he could see the Lord "high and lofty." He had to come to the end of himself before there could be a new beginning.

The point is God usually has to allow us to go through the deep surgery of detachment from every idolatrous attachment in order to empty our thrones so he alone can fill them. There seems to be no other way. Generally, we don't really see God, really seek after God and find him, until we have tried almost every possible other way and found it empty. Only when we reach the place of utter desperation, when we have exhausted all our own resources, do we turn to God. It is usually only when some King Uzziah dies, when some false idol is smashed and broken and we are in a position of humility and extremity, that we turn our eyes toward God.

John Wesley's Georgia Fiasco

Given the experience of our founder, John Wesley, we United Methodists should understand this necessary emptying. Wesley had an awful experience as a missionary in Georgia. In his zeal and self-righteousness he embarked for Georgia in October, 1735, hoping to convert the Native Americans and minister to the colonists. But what an utter failure he was!

He had only a few opportunities to preach; and when he did, the Native Americans were almost totally unresponsive. Among the colonists he didn't fare much better. They weren't quite sure what to make of the seriousness with which he approached religion. In his efforts to involve them in spiritual disciplines and to maintain church order, he appeared to them as rigid, bigoted, and tactless. Finally, because of Wesley's own clumsiness, the situation got completely out of hand. With legal proceedings staring him in the face, he fled in disgust and indignation, boarding a ship to return home to England.

What a bleak, depressing voyage that must have been! As the ship was nearing England's shore, Wesley reviewed his catastrophic Georgia experience in his Journal: "I went to Georgia to convert the Indians; but oh, who on earth will convert me? Who, what is he that will deliver me from this evil heart of unbelief?"[1]

As a result of his utter failure, Wesley was at the end of his spiritual tether. The house of his self-made righteousness had come crashing down. But now that his self-reliance and self-sufficiency had been shattered, Wesley was finally at a place where he was ready to trust in Christ, and Christ *alone*, for salvation. Before Georgia he trusted in Jesus and John Wesley. After Georgia he trusted in Jesus alone.

Yet without the debacle of Georgia, there would have never been the miracle of Aldersgate. Only when Wesley had been emptied of his own righteousness could he be filled with the righteousness of Christ.

Will Decline Lead to Humility?

What do Isaiah's and Wesley's experiences have to do with our present situation as United Methodists today? Simply this: if there is going to be a renewal of holiness of heart and life among us, it will only happen as we allow ourselves to be broken and humbled, and as we cry out in desperation to God. Fenelon said, "The work of God can be built only upon the ruins of ourselves."

Perhaps during the past few decades, God has been working to bring us to a place where in humility and desperation we would cry out to him. Compared to other periods in our church's history, this has not been a very exciting time to be a United Methodist! The glory days of most of our congregations are somewhere in the distant past.

The denomination has been declining in numbers for twenty-five years now—from more than 11 million members in 1964 to fewer than 9 million in 1989. Our Sunday school attendance is just half of what it was in 1964. If we focus on one of those years, 1985, for example, we get a clearer picture of what's been happening. In 1985 we lost a total of 75,692 members. That works out to a loss of 1,455 persons a week. Or to think of it in another way, it's as if we closed a church of 207 members every day during that year.[2]

But more important than the decline in numbers is what the decline reflects: a loss of spiritual vitality and an inability to win new converts and make new disciples. Let's face it, the average United Methodist congregation today seems to have very little drawing power. When people visit our churches, can they sense an air of expectancy in the worshiping congregation? Do they leave knowing they have been in the presence of God? We have become sterile, unable to reproduce ourselves, unable to hold onto our youth. Our church no longer has the influence on American culture that it once did.

It is not uncommon these days to lament the sorry state of

our denominational and congregational life. "Methodist bashing" has become popular in some quarters. So you may be thinking, "Not again. Not another reciting of the woeful litany of decline. Not another effort to parade all our dirty laundry. Hasn't there been enough of that?" Yes, there has.

What is important now is that, having been made painfully aware of the graveness of our situation, we allow that awareness to create in us a poverty of spirit, a humility which will drive us out of ourselves to seek God. This period of decline can result in new life if it brings us back to God. After Peter denied his Lord, he "went out and wept bitterly" (Luke 22:62). But his tears and failure shattered his false self-sufficiency and caused him to depend on God. On the other hand, this period can lead us to despair and death if, in our stubbornness, we persist in our self-reliance. After Judas had betrayed Jesus he "went and hanged himself" (Matt. 27:5). He would have been forgiven and restored if he had turned to Christ in humility and repentance. But his failure, instead of driving him to God, drove him to the final act of self-destruction. Which will it be for us? Will we humble ourselves and turn to God? Or will we cling to the notion that things really aren't as bad as they seem and that eventually we will be able to fix the situation and turn things around? Will decline lead to humility and brokenness before God? Or will it lead to hardness of heart and further rationalization? Will we close our minds and confirm ourselves in our proud resistance?

Let's Stop Blaming Others

"In the year that King Uzziah *died*, I saw the Lord." If our decline is going to produce in us a posture of humility, I believe there are certain attitudes to which we must die.

We must die to the tendency to blame someone else for the mess we are in. It is easy to point fingers—at the bishops, the general boards and agencies, the theological seminaries, the annual conferences, the special interest groups, the pastors, the laity. You can pin the blame on any of them and make a good case that that particular group is the source of our problem.

At present we United Methodists are like a big dysfunctional family. In dysfunctional families there are no innocent parties. Each member contributes to the dysfunction in some way. There is therefore no point in constantly throwing stones at the other members of the family, castigating them for how bad off we are. That can become a subtle smokescreen keeping us from the work *we* need to do if our dysfunction is to be healed.

Each of us needs to recognize the part we play in the dysfunction and start taking responsibility by admitting, "It's not my brother or my sister . . . not the bishops or the boards, not the pastors or the laity . . . it's *me*, O Lord, standing in the need of prayer."

Isaiah cried out "Woe is *me*. . . . I am a man of unclean lips, and I live among a people of unclean lips" (Isa. 6:5). Oh, that each of us—whatever group in the church we are a part of—would likewise cry out! Oh, that a spirit of repentance would fall upon us! Each of us needs to pray with the Psalmist, "Search *me*, O God, and know my heart. . . . See if there is any wicked way in *me*" (Ps. 139:23-24).

We have keen eyes to see the wicked ways of others, but we are blind to our own ways. We need to stop shifting the blame and start asking God to show us where we are responsible. And then, in relation to the wicked ways of others, we need to stop accusing and start interceding.

Methodist Pride

"In the year that King Uzziah *died*, I saw the Lord." If decline is going to lead to humility, we also need to die to "Methodist pride." This pride manifests itself in a number of ways, but it can be seen most of all in our stubbornness and unwillingness to admit that we can't fix the situation we are in, that we can't solve our problems ourselves.

Several years ago Charles Ferguson wrote a history of American Methodism entitled *Organizing to Beat the Devil*.[3] The title expresses what we Methodists have done so well for more than two hundred years—organize. All one has to do is examine the *Book of Discipline* or attend an Annual Conference or a Charge Conference to realize that. As William Willimon and Robert Wilson have observed, sometimes the size of our flow charts makes even our small, family-like congregations look like General Motors.[4]

There is no question that throughout our history God has worked effectively through our structures and our organization. Wesley placed people into societies, classes, and bands. Spiritual growth occurred. Francis Asbury developed an itinerant system for appointing preachers. Churches were planted all across the frontier. The story of the growth of American Methodism is the story of how faith and form came together to spread across an emerging nation. We United Methodists understand the value of organization. The word *method* is a part of our name!

However, when we are good at something, it is very tempting to begin idolizing it, relying on it instead of on God. That's why when we United Methodists are faced with a problem, it's very easy for us to look to an organizational solution for the answer instead of looking to God. We think, "If we could just shuffle things around, if we could just reorganize, that would make things right."

Thinking that way makes us feel good about ourselves. After all, when we are organizing, *we* are the chief actors, *we* are the ones in control, *we* are the ones doing the work so we can take the credit when the job gets done. So if one organizational solution doesn't work, we try another and then another and another. For as long as we keep trying, we can cling to the notion that *we* can fix it; we can do it *ourselves*.

The truth is, of course, that all the organizing in the world cannot create spiritual renewal or a passion for holiness anymore than a fireplace can create a fire. Only God can create those things. Isaiah, as we shall see, needed a touch from God to be renewed. So do we.

Organizing can, however, help to shape and sustain spiritual passion once it has been brought into existence. Fires need fireplaces to contain them and to channel their heat. But when we make organization a substitute for what only God can create, all we have is a cold, damp fireplace which may look nice, but will never provide warmth and heat.

There is a humorous story about an old man who cut his finger and went to the local clinic to see if he needed stitches. When he entered the clinic there were two doors, one marked "Over 65," the other marked "Under 65." So he went through the door marked "Over 65." He found himself in another room, again facing two doors. One was marked "Male," the other marked "Female." He went through the door marked "Male" and to his chagrin found himself again in a room with two doors in front of him, one marked "Internal" and the other marked "External." He looked at his cut finger. "I guess it's external," he thought. So he went through that door. This time he found himself in another room, again with two doors, the one marked "Major" and the other marked "Minor." He walked through the door marked "Minor" only to find himself back out on the street!

When he got home, his wife asked, "Did they help you at the clinic?"

"No," he replied, "but they sure were well organized!"

Too many United Methodist congregations are like that clinic. People look at them and say, "They sure are well organized." But they have come through the front doors of our sanctuaries and gone out our back doors without being made whole.

We must die to the notion that we can organize our way out of decline. Let's admit that we can't fix it. Although organizational strategies are useful, they can only harness and direct a renewed passion for holiness; they cannot create it. Only God can. But if we will humble ourselves and pray and seek his face; if we will acknowledge our utter helplessness to turn ourselves and our congregations around, God will renew us again.

In the face of a great army which was about to attack the nation of Israel, King Jehoshaphat—Uzziah's grandfather—prayed a prayer that should be on the lips of every United Methodist today: "O Lord. . . . We do not know what to do, but our eyes are on you" (II Chron. 20:6, 12). When we turn our eyes away from ourselves, when we die to what we are trusting in, like Isaiah in the year that King Uzziah died, we too shall see the Lord.

Notes

1. *Works*, 1, p. 74.
2. William H. Willimon and Robert L. Wilson, *Rekindling the Flame* (Nashville: Abingdon Press, 1987), p. 12.
3. Charles W. Ferguson, *Organizing to Beat the Devil* (Garden City, N.Y.: Doubleday, 1971).
4. Willimon and Wilson, *Rekindling the Flame*, p. 88.

3

A Vision of a Holy God

"In the year that King Uzziah died," says Isaiah, "I *saw the Lord*." While he was worshiping in the temple, Isaiah had a vision of God. But what in his vision caused such a profound effect upon him? What did he see? What did he fully comprehend about God for the first time?

It can be summed up in one word, which the seraphs, the heavenly beings around God's throne, repeated three times: "Holy, holy, holy." Above all, Isaiah got a glimpse of the holiness of God. It became clear to him as never before that God is *holy*.

Now at first we may have a difficult time understanding the significance of this. We said earlier that the prophet's experience in Isaiah 6 is positioned where it is to answer the question that is raised in chapters 1–5: how can an unholy people become a holy people? But what kind of answer is this? What sort of a solution to that problem? Why a vision of God?

We can understand that humility is necessary if there is to be a renewal of holiness among God's people, but why a vision of the holiness of God? Why is that necessary? The question is how the *people* of God can become holy. The problem then is not with God but with them. So why this focus on God's holiness? Why not focus directly on theirs?

This part of Isaiah's solution to the problem may seem strange to us. We want something practical, down to earth, something we can *do*. What Isaiah offers us is profoundly theological—a vision of heaven.

Yet when compared with other Scriptures, Isaiah's solution does not seem unusual at all. In fact, it is typical of the whole Bible. Throughout the Scripture, God's holiness is always seen as the source and the basis for ours. The call to holiness in I Peter expresses it well: "As he who called you is holy, be holy yourselves in all your conduct: for it is written, 'You shall be holy, for I am holy' " (1:15-16).

The holiness of God's people is always defined and determined by the holiness of God. Our holiness is seen as a reflection of God's. Furthermore, it is only when we get a glimpse of *God's* holiness that we begin to feel the force of the imperative laid upon us: *you* shall be holy.

Any call then to holiness among the people of God must begin with a call to consider first the holiness of God. That is what Isaiah needed. That is what Israel, the people of God, needed. That is what we, the people called United Methodist, need. If there is going to be a recovery of and passion for holiness of heart and life in our church and our congregations, we need not only a spirit of humility, but also a fresh vision of the holiness of God.

But what is the holiness of God? As we work our way through Isaiah 6, we will discover that here, as in other parts of the Bible, the holiness of God does not have a precisely defined, exact meaning. It is not something which is narrowly conceived but is closely linked with a number of other divine attributes or characteristics. Holiness is not merely one attribute of God which is distinct from God's other attributes. It is the outshining of all that God is. Theologian R. A. Finlayson describes it well: "As the sun's rays, containing all the colors of the spectrum, come together and blend into light, so all the attributes of God come together in His self-manifestation and blend into holiness."[1]

All this, of course, has profound implications for us as the people of God. We are to be holy *as God is holy*. If, then, God's holiness is inclusive of a number of divine characteristics or attributes, the meaning of holiness in our lives should not be narrowly conceived or understood either. When it is—and sometimes it has been—the "beauty of holiness" (Ps. 29:2; 96:9) will be distorted or obscured.

Thus for each divine characteristic or attribute associated in Isaiah's vision with the holiness of God, there is a corresponding characteristic in the life of the holy people of God. Each of these corresponding characteristics reflects an essential element of holiness. Along with the other characteristics, it blends together to constitute holiness of heart and life in all its fullness. Each then must be taken into account if we are to behold the many-splendored beauty of holiness.

What are the divine characteristics or attributes that confronted Isaiah in his vision and caused the seraphs to cry "Holy, holy, holy"? In the rest of this chapter and the four chapters that follow, we will consider each one. And in each case we will draw out their implications for holiness of heart and life among God's people today.

God's Unrivaled Majesty

"In the year that King Uzziah died, I saw the Lord sitting on a throne, *high and lofty*" (Isa. 6:1). At the very beginning of his description of his vision of God, Isaiah emphasizes God's separateness, God's transcendence over all creation and all that is not God. The Lord *alone* is the high and lofty One.

This is a recurring theme throughout the book of Isaiah.

For example, in Isaiah 2:12 the prophet declares, "For the Lord of hosts has a day against all that is proud and lofty, against all that is lifted up and high." Then he describes God as going on a campaign to bring not only proud people down to size, but anything else that appears tall—fortified walls, ships on the sea, even stately trees and large mountains. On that day, Isaiah concludes, "the Lord alone will be exalted" (2:17).

In his vision, the way Isaiah describes God's appearance also underscores God's separateness. He sees nothing higher than the hem of God's robe! His description is similar to other Old Testament accounts in which persons are said to have seen God. For instance, when Moses and the elders of Israel "saw the God of Israel," all they saw was the pavement under God's feet (Exod. 24:9-10).

The action of the seraphs, the heavenly beings around God's throne, further stresses the immense distance which separates God from all creatures. "Each had six wings: with two they covered their faces, and with two they covered their feet, and with two they flew" (Isa. 6:2). By covering their faces, the seraphs recognize that because of the infinite distance between them, they as creatures are not permitted to look upon the Creator. Even heavenly beings, the highest of creatures, dare not do that. By covering their feet they also acknowledge that their common parts should not be casually displayed in the presence of the Creator.

To say God is holy is to declare there is, to use Søren Kierkegaard's expression, an "infinite qualitative difference" between the creature and the Creator, the human and the divine. Indeed, there is an absolute gulf fixed between them which cannot be crossed. As theologian Emil Brunner puts it: "The borderline which separates the nature of God from all other forms of existence . . . is not only a frontier line, it is a *closed* frontier."[2]

A People Set Apart

The fact that God is holy means that God is separate from all creation. He is high and lifted up. What in our lives as people of God corresponds to this aspect of the holiness of God? Obviously, we cannot be separate from creation in the same way in which God is, for we are a part of creation itself. But a call to the people of God runs throughout the Scriptures, encouraging us to separate ourselves from the values and life-style of those around us. If we are to be holy as God is holy, we must be responsive to this call.

Again and again throughout the Old Testament, God commands the people of Israel to be separate from the people of the surrounding nations. They are not to intermarry with them or to worship their false gods or imitate their practices (Deut. 7:1-6; 12:29-32; 18:9-14). And what is the basis for this call to separation? It is bound up with the holiness of God: "You shall be *holy* to me; for I the Lord am *holy,* and I have *separated* you from the other peoples to be mine" (Lev. 20:26; cf. Deut. 7:6).

In the New Testament we find Paul reiterating the call to separation in his appeal to the Christians at Corinth not to be "mismatched with unbelievers" (II Cor. 6:14). As a part of the patchwork of quotations which he draws from the Old Testament to substantiate his appeal, he includes these words: "Therefore come out from them, and be separate from them, says the Lord, and touch nothing unclean" (6:17). Finally he places his particular call to separation within the context of the call to holiness: "Since we have these promises, beloved, let us cleanse ourselves from every defilement of body and of spirit, *making holiness perfect* in the fear of God" (7:1). Elsewhere in the New Testament the call to separation can also be heard in the more general appeals for Christians not to love the world or be conformed to its value system (Rom. 12:2; James 4:4; I John 2:15-17).

Unfortunately some Christians throughout history have made holiness of heart and life synonymous with separation—as if separation in and of itself constituted holiness. Often those who have made this mistake have also narrowly defined separation merely as abstinence from certain habits and practices—such as smoking, drinking, and card-playing. Holiness is then reduced to avoiding the activities on their particular list of taboos. It becomes a code word for what a Christian *doesn't* do. Some of our early Methodist forbears fell into this sort of thinking.

But it is also a mistake to think that we can be holy apart from separation. When that happens it becomes difficult to tell the difference between Christians and non-Christians. While some early Methodists made the mistake of reducing holiness to separation, we make the mistake of seeking holiness without separation.

The findings of a recent study of United Methodist congregational life by our General Board of Discipleship bear this out.[3] The study shows that United Methodists today are being shaped more by the values of American culture than by the values of their Christian faith. According to Ray Sells, a board consultant and part of the team that did the research, the study indicates that "the values in the marketplace have more power to shape people's lives than the values of the Christian faith." Moreover, people are bringing those marketplace values into the church "for affirmation, not challenge."[4]

Most disturbing is the explanation the study offers for this situation: "Most people don't expect the congregation to help them connect their Christian faith to daily life. Many members don't understand that this connection is important or necessary to genuine Christian discipleship."[5]

It is obvious that we United Methodists have been doing a poor job of identifying the frontier lines that exist between the church and the world. There may have been a time in our distant past when we were drawing too many lines—and sometimes in the wrong places. But now we have gone to the opposite extreme—not drawing any lines—to the extent that our congregations don't expect us to draw lines at all!

We need to sound the call to separation once again. There will not be a renewal of holiness of heart and life among us until we do.

Separation from the Attachment to Things

What are the specific areas in which we as individuals and congregations need to be challenged to separation from the culture around us? What particular issues of our day need to be addressed? We could speak about many, but let us simply focus upon one: we need to call our congregations to be separate from the materialistic mindset that pervades our culture.

In America today the pursuit of happiness has almost become synonymous with the pursuit of money and possessions. Greed, which used to be one of the seven deadly sins, has been transposed into a virtue. In the movie *Wall Street*, Michael Douglas, as a rapacious stock trader, Gordon Gekko, boldly proclaims the gospel of our culture. "Greed is American," he declares unashamedly. "Greed is good. Greed can save our country."

We live in a culture that worships at the altars of consumerism. Its temples are shopping malls. Its priests and priestesses are Madison Avenue executives. Its sermons are television commercials. Its saints are people with six-figure incomes. Its annual pilgrimage is the Christmas shopping season. Its logos are designer labels.

This pervasive spirit of our age is alive and well in our congregations. It is there when we measure success by the size of our church budget or the cost of our building program. It is there when one's influence in a congregation can be gauged by the size of one's financial contribution. It is there when a salary scale, not dedication and service, is the determining factor in pastoral appointments.

John White contends that, across the spectrum, materialism has become the golden cow, the false god worshiped in the American church. "Evangelical churches," he says, "fundamentalist churches, liberal Protestant and Catholic churches are full of people who have gone through some form of Christianization (be it baptism or going forward) but whom we have taught to trust in dollars and in technology more than in the ascended Christ."[6]

Today as never before, pastors must challenge church members, both individually and collectively, to be separate, different from the surrounding culture in their attitudes toward property and possessions. Congregations need to grapple long and hard with what the Bible teaches about wealth and possessions. Then what the Bible says—not what the culture says—can begin to inform their thinking as they are faced with varied and often complex decisions related to money.

Members of the earliest Christian congregation described in the book of Acts did not cling to their property and possessions, but held them lightly. They were even willing to sell what they had to meet the needs of others in their community (Acts 2:44-45). What would happen today if Christians began to reflect a similar attitude?

Several years ago Tom Skinner, the black evangelist, was in a large business building in New York City. He was on the elevator going down to the ground floor when a man—the only other person in the elevator—pulled a gun and ordered Tom to give him his wallet. So Tom took his wallet out of his back pocket and handed it to the man.

But a few moments later, as the elevator was grinding to a stop, Tom said to the man, "Listen, what you probably want is my money, and I never carry my money in my wallet. I always carry it in my pocket." Then he pulled a small wad of bills out of his pocket and said, "Here, take this too."

The man was so shocked by what Tom had done that as the elevator door opened he simply dropped the wallet he was holding and ran, not even bothering to take the money Tom was offering him.

Several days later, Tom was eating at a restaurant in the same vicinity when who should walk in and sit down at the counter but the man who had held him up on the elevator. After a while Tom went over and sat next to him. "Remember me?" Tom said, smiling. From the expression on the man's face you would have thought he had seen a ghost!

"How in the world could I forget!" he exclaimed. Then when he had calmed down he asked, "Tell me, why did you do what you did? You knew there was no money in your wallet, but I didn't. So why didn't you just let me take off with it. Why did you offer me your money as well?"

Tom Skinner smiled. Then he looked the man straight in the eye, "Because I wanted you to know that I'm not attached to my money."

To be holy is to be separate, not attached to the things to which this world clings, so that we can be free to be attached to God. What does the world around us see when it looks at our congregations? Does it see a holy people—separate, distinct, governed by a radically different set of values? Or does it only see a reflection of itself?

Notes

1. R. A. Finlayson, *The Holiness of God* (Glasgow: Pickering and Inglis, 1955), p. 5.
2. Emil Brunner, *The Christian Doctrine of God* (Philadelphia: Westminster, 1950), p. 159.
3. "Study Says UM's Don't Live Their Faith in Everyday Life," *The United Methodist Reporter* (July 6, 1990), p. 1.
4. Ibid.
5. Ibid.
6. John White, *The Golden Cow* (Downers Grove, Ill.: InterVarsity Press, 1979), p. 159.

4

Opening Ourselves to God's Presence

A vision of a holy God! That is what is needed for unholy people to be transformed into holy people. So Isaiah's experience would tell us. But what does a vision of the holiness of God mean? What did it mean for Isaiah, and what will it mean for us? We want to know.

When Isaiah was given a vision of the holiness of God not only did he see God high and exalted, but he also saw the glory of God. "Holy, holy, holy, is the Lord of hosts," cry the seraphs, "the whole earth is full of his *glory*" (Isa. 6:3). It is the meaning and significance of this aspect of the holiness of God—holiness as glory—that we want to consider in this chapter.

God's Glorious Radiance

According to *A Theological Word Book of the Bible*, the glory of God is "the term used to express that which men can *apprehend*, originally by sight of the presence of God on earth."[1] A good synonym for *glory* is *presence*. That's why the

New Jewish Version of the Old Testament often uses the word *presence* to translate the Hebrew word *kabod* (glory).

When the Bible says "the glory of the Lord filled the temple" (II Chron. 7:1) or "the glory of the Lord shone around them" (Luke 2:9) it means that at those times there was a visible manifestation of the presence of God. Those who were there *knew* that God was present!

Not only in Isaiah's vision, but throughout the Scriptures the glory of God is closely associated with the holiness of God. For example, after Israel's deliverance at the Red Sea, Moses exclaims, "Who is like you, majestic in *holiness*, awesome in *glory*, doing wonders?" (Exod. 15:11). Later, when God is giving Moses instructions concerning the tabernacle, the two are linked again. Concerning the altar at the entrance to the tabernacle where sacrifices are to be offered, God says, "I will meet with the Israelites there, and it shall be *sanctified* [made holy] by my *glory*" (Exod. 29:43).

What does this close association between glory and holiness tell us about holiness? In his discussion of the holiness of God, theologian Emil Brunner suggests that there are two "movements" in divine holiness.[2] The first is a movement of withdrawal and exclusion: God separates himself, sets himself apart from creation. We dealt with that movement in the last chapter when we discussed God's separateness and transcendence. Usually when we think of holiness, this is the movement that comes to mind.

But there is a second movement of holiness—expansion and inclusion—which we often fail to take into account. This movement seems to contradict the first, but actually it completes and fulfills it. For as the Holy One, God wills to be recognized as holy. Not content simply to *be* holy, God desires to *make* holy. God wants the whole earth to be filled with his glory.

Out of God's holiness emerges a desire to communicate

with his creation. Because God is holy, he does not want to be distant from creation, but longs for fellowship and relationship with it. So God moves out of himself seeking to share himself with creation and to be recognized by it.

God's glory, then, which is the result of that movement toward us, is an expression of his holiness. It is, as Johann Bengel, the eighteenth-century biblical scholar, so aptly put it, "holiness uncovered."[3]

A People Who Seek God's Presence

But what does this mean for the people of God? If we are to be holy as God is holy, what implications will this aspect of holiness—holiness as glory—have for us both as individuals and congregations? Simply this: *a holy people will be a people who are increasingly open to the presence of God and constantly seeking after it.*

God wills to make himself known. He wants the whole earth to be filled with his glory. He is looking for those who will be receptive to his overtures. God is looking for a people who will be present to him.

God, of course, is present everywhere at all times. "Where can I go from your spirit? Or where can I flee from your presence?" exclaims the Psalmist. "If I ascend to heaven, you are there; if I make my bed in Sheol, you are there. If I take the wings of the morning and settle at the farthest limits of the sea, even there your hand shall lead me, and your right hand shall hold me fast" (139:8-10). God presence is inescapable. When we try to run from him we run right into him.

But although God is everywhere present—the whole earth *is* full of his glory!—not everyone is aware of God's presence. Jacob had a dream in which God spoke to him. He saw angels ascending and descending upon a ladder which connected heaven and earth. When he awoke from his dream he cried out, "Surely the Lord is in this place—and I did not know it!" (Gen. 28:16). That was his problem. Often it is ours. God is present all the time, but we are unaware of it.

So God's presence should not be equated with our awareness of God's presence. God is present whether we are aware of it or not, but his presence is made manifest only when we are aware of it. That is why the Psalmist exhorts God's people to "seek the Lord and his strength; seek his presence continually" (Ps. 105:4). The Psalmist is concerned that the people come to an awareness of God's presence— and such an awareness does not automatically follow from the fact that God is present everywhere. God's presence must be *sought*. We must become receptive to it. God is always present to us, but in order for his presence to have its full impact upon our lives, we must learn to be present to God.

A holy people, then, are a people who are increasingly open to God's presence and forever seeking after it. Once again the Psalmist expresses the responsive attitude that ought to characterize God's holy people: "When thou saidst, Seek ye my face; my heart said unto thee, Thy face, Lord, will I seek" (Ps. 27:8 KJV).

Seeking God's Presence in the Likely Places

How do we seek God? What must we do, both as individuals and as congregations, if we are to cultivate receptivity and responsiveness to God's presence? First and foremost, we must learn to seek God in the places where he has told us to seek him.

Thank God he has not left us in the dark about how we should seek his presence. There are some places where God has promised to meet us. John Wesley called these divinely appointed places "the means of grace."[4] These, he said, are the "ordinary channels" through which God conveys his presence to us. They are the "likely places" where God meets us.

According to Wesley, Christ himself instituted five such means of grace for us. In the "Large Minutes,"[5] which contained Wesley's plan of discipline for the early Methodists, he discusses each of them briefly:

1. *Prayer*. Of all the means of grace, prayer is "the grand means of drawing near to God."[6] The others are meaningful only when they are combined with or lead us to prayer. Prayer is also the most all-encompassing of the means. It includes confession of sin, petition for our own needs, intercession for the needs of others, and thanksgiving for God's goodness and mercy. It embraces our lives as individuals (private prayer), families (family prayer), and congregations (public prayer). Prayer is to be engaged in at all times—morning, evening and throughout the day.

2. *Searching the Scriptures*. We are to read the Bible constantly (every day), regularly (in an orderly fashion), carefully (using study helps), seriously (beginning and ending with prayer), and fruitfully (immediately putting into practice what we have learned). In addition to reading the Bible, searching the Scriptures involves meditating upon them, and hearing them preached and taught.

3. *Attendance at the Lord's Supper*. Christ is made known to us in the breaking of the bread (Luke 24:35). Through the sacrament of Holy Communion, his real presence is conveyed to us through the Holy Spirit. Therefore, it is "the duty of every Christian to receive the Lord's Supper as often as he can."[7]

4. *Fasting*. Because fasting weans the soul from its attachment to the things of this world and increases spiritual sensitivity, Jesus commended the practice to his disciples

(Matt. 6:16-18). Wesley, likewise, encouraged the Methodists to fast. He was convinced that "when you seek God with fasting added to prayer, you cannot seek His face in vain."[8] Methodists generally observed Friday as a fast day.

5. *Christian Conference.* "For where two or three are gathered in my name, I am there among them" (Matt. 18:20). Wesley used this text to prove that gathering together in some form of small-group structure is necessary for believers. It too is a means of grace instituted by Christ. As believers gather together for fellowship, encouragement, accountability, study, and service the risen Christ is present in their midst. Although the particular form of the small-group structure may vary, some form is essential for growth in grace.

According to Wesley these five means of grace are the divinely appointed places of waiting. If we are going to seek God's presence, we should devote ourselves to them.

Wesley's five means of grace parallel the description of the activities of the earliest Christian congregation in Acts 2:42: "They devoted themselves to the apostles' teaching [searching the Scriptures] and fellowship [Christian conference], to the breaking of bread [attendance at the Lord's Supper] and the prayers [prayer]." If we add to this the description of the congregation at Antioch (Acts 13:1-3) which was "worshiping the Lord and fasting," then we see that all five of Wesley's means of grace were an integral part of the life and practice of the earliest Christians.

But are they enough a part of our life and practice today? As we seek to be open and receptive to the divine presence, are we, like the early Christians and early Methodists, devoting ourselves to these things? How faithful is the average United Methodist congregation today in observing the means of grace?

Are we a people of prayer? How much time do we as

individuals spend in prayer each day? Do we pray together with our families? Is our church sanctuary a house of prayer? Do we know what it means to persevere in prayer as together we seek God's will for our congregations? Are prayer meetings, prayer groups, prayer vigils, prayer chains, and prayer partners a part of our congregational life?

Are we a people of the Bible? Do we read the Bible every day? Are we engaged in serious study of it? Are the Scriptures read and expounded in our worship services? Are there regular opportunities for Bible study in our church? Are we committed to the authority of Scripture in ordering our individual and congregational life? Are we doers of the word as well as hearers?

Are we a people of the Eucharist? Do we gather at the Lord's table regularly and often? Do we look forward to Communion Sundays? Do we expect Christ to be present? Are our congregations instructed in the meaning of Holy Communion?

Are we a people who fast? Do we understand the purpose and value of fasting? Do we engage in it regularly or from time to time? Are there regular times and seasons when our pastors encourage us to fast?

Are we a people who are committed to small-group structures? Do we recognize the necessity of small groups for our growth in grace? Are we accountable to a group for our practice of spiritual disciplines? Are there share groups, prayer groups, accountability groups, study groups, action groups in our church?

If there is to be a renewal of holiness of heart and life among the people called United Methodist, if we are to be a holy people, open and receptive to the divine presence, we must devote ourselves to the means of grace. There is no other way! These are places where God has instructed us to seek him if we desire to find him.

Yet, you might ask, "How in the world is this ever going to

happen in our congregation? So many of our members are nominal in their commitment and have little or no interest in any of the means of grace we have been thinking about. How will they ever get serious about these things?"

Many, in fact the majority, probably never will get serious about them. The cost of commitment is too great; the price is too high. But that should not cause us to despair. We should concentrate instead on the minority of people in our congregation who are serious about their commitment to Christ. We should find the people in the congregation who are genuinely seeking God's presence and organize them into groups. Let them voluntarily commit themselves to the practice of the means of grace at a level appropriate for them. Let them come together once a week for study, prayer, fellowship, and accountability. The Covenant Discipleship program, modeled after the early Methodist class meetings and produced by the United Methodist Board of Discipleship, could be used to help facilitate these groups.

This strategy is workable in any local congregation, from the smallest to the largest. It is essentially the strategy Wesley himself used in working for renewal in the Church of England. On a large scale, he created a society (the Methodists) within a church (the Church of England). On a smaller scale, we can create societies—small groups of those who are seriously seeking holiness of heart and life—within our local churches. The spiritual fervor of these groups can spark renewal in the life of the whole congregation.

Finding God's Presence in Unlikely Places

But not only are we to seek God's presence through the means of grace—the likely places where God has told us he will meet us. We are to seek God in unlikely places too. For although God has designated some places where he will convey his presence to us, God is not limited to those places. God is all-present and can manifest his presence anytime and anywhere. If we are attentive, every moment, every experience of life, no matter how mundane it might seem, can become a channel of the divine presence. "The *whole earth* is full of his glory."

Elizabeth Barrett Browning's poem expresses this truth well:

> Earth's crammed with heaven,
> And every common bush afire with God;
> But only he who sees takes off his shoes,
> The rest sit around it and pluck blackberries.

Those who are seeking holiness of heart and life have learned to take off their shoes! They are open and receptive to the presence of God, and are learning to find his presence in unlikely places.

Where are some unlikely places we should seek his presence? We will briefly mention two.

First, we can seek his presence in the ordinary, humdrum, affairs of life. Brother Lawrence, the seventeenth-century Carmelite friar, made this the chief ambition of his life. He sought to "practice the presence of God" in the midst of all his everyday activities. He came to the place where he could say, "The time of business does not with me differ from the time of prayer, and in the noise and clatter of my kitchen, while several persons are at the same time calling for different things, I possess God in as great tranquility as if I were upon my knees at the blessed sacrament."[9]

We too can learn to practice the presence of God. Each moment, each experience of life, no matter how dull or ordinary, can become an epiphany of divine grace if we learn to be attentive to God. So in the midst of all our activities we must learn to pray, "Lord, you are present here. Make me aware of your presence."

Second, we can seek God's presence in the face of human need. In the parable of the last judgment, both the sheep and the goats—those who were received and those who were rejected—were puzzled and surprised: "Lord, when was it that we saw you hungry or thirsty or a stranger or naked or sick or in prison?" (Matt. 25:44). He had been there all along, yet they had failed to see him. But where was he? Then the answer came: "As you did it to one of the least of these, you did it to me."

Christ meets us in the faces of the poor, the broken, the hungry, the lonely, the disenfranchised. So Mother Teresa of Calcutta tells us that when she holds a dying leper in her arms, she sees the face of Christ. He meets her there. As she ministers to the broken and the dying she ministers to him.[10]

In the face of human need, our natural tendency is to turn and look the other way. Like the priest and the Levite who came upon the beaten man on the Jericho road, we want to "pass by on the other side" (Luke 10:31-32). Jesus would say to us, "Don't turn away from human need. Don't keep your distance. Reach out and touch it. Look deep into the eyes of your hurting sisters or brothers. Look closely and you'll see me looking back at you."

As God's people, called to be holy as he is holy, we seek his presence in the likely places—through the means of grace, the places God has promised to meet us. But we also seek God's presence in the unlikely places—through our commonplace everyday activities, in the face of human need.

Are we open to God's presence? Are we seeking it as we should? How is God calling us to seek his presence now?

Notes

1. L. H. Brockington, "Presence," in *A Theological Word Book of the Bible*, ed. by Alan Richardson (New York: Macmillan, 1950), p. 175.

2. Emil Brunner, *The Christian Doctrine of God* (Philadelphia: Westminster, 1950), pp. 162-64.
3. Cited in Edmund Jacob, *Theology of the Old Testament*, trans. Arthur W. Heathcote and Philip J. Allcock (London: Hodder and Stoughton, 1958), pp. 79-80.
4. See Wesley's sermon, "The Means of Grace," in *Works*, 5, pp. 185-201.
5. *Works*, 8, pp. 322-23.
6. *Letters*, IV, p. 90.
7. *Works*, 7, p. 147.
8. *Letters*, V, p. 112.
9. Nicholas Hermann (Brother Lawrence), *The Practice of the Presence of God* (Old Tappan, N.J.: Fleming H. Revell Co., 1958), p. 29.
10. See Malcolm Muggeridge, *Something Beautiful for God* (London: Collins/Fontana Books, 1972).

5

A People of Power

A holy people. Called to be holy *as God is holy*. We are letting Isaiah's vision of the holiness of God tell us what that means. God's holiness is his majesty, his separateness from all creation. We, then, are to be a people separate from the world and its value system. God's holiness is his glorious radiance. So we are to be a people open to God's presence and always seeking it. That's what we've learned so far. Now we want to consider a third aspect of God's holiness and its implications for the people of God: holiness as power.

God's Infinite Power

In Isaiah's vision there is a close association between God's holiness and God's power. Isaiah sees God "sitting on a throne" (Isa. 6:1)—an expression which implies that God is a king. Later he exclaims, "My eyes have seen the King, the Lord of hosts!" (v. 5). In Isaiah's day and time a king's power was absolute. All might and authority rested in his hands. The king *was* the government. Seeing God as a king sitting on a throne underscores God's absolute sovereignty and power. Twice in Isaiah's vision, God is described as "the Lord of hosts" (vv. 3, 5). According to Old Testament scholar Otto Kaiser, this title, which is used for God more than sixty times in the book of Isaiah, is an affirmation that "the holy God, the Lord over all the powers and forces which form and control this world, possesses the power to make his will prevail in the world."[1]

God's power is also conveyed in Isaiah's vision by the thunderous voices of the seraphs, which cause the doorposts of the temple to shake, and by the smoke which fills the sanctuary (Isa. 6:4). The prophet's description is similar to the description of the meeting of God and the people of Israel on Mount Sinai when they were given the Ten Commandments (Exod. 19:16-19). On that occasion, the lightning and thunder, the smoke, and the trembling of the mountain created the same awesome sense of God's infinite power.

What we find in Isaiah's vision—the linking of God's holiness and power—is characteristic of the entire Old Testament. For example, in his song of praise following God's deliverance of Israel at the Red Sea, Moses extols the power of God: "Your right hand, O Lord, glorious in power—your right hand, O Lord, shattered the enemy" (Exod. 15:6). His awareness of God's power then causes him to exalt God's holiness: "Who is like you, O Lord, among the gods? Who is like you, *majestic in holiness*, awesome in splendor, doing wonders? You stretched out your right hand, the earth swallowed them" (vv. 11-12).

Likewise in I Samuel 6 there is a demonstration of God's power when God slays seventy men of the village of Bethshemesh "because they looked into the ark of the Lord" (v. 19). The ark had been captured by the Philistines, but it was sent back to Israel because of the plagues which came upon the Philistines as a result of its presence in their midst. The people of Bethshemesh rejoiced when they saw the ark but aroused God's anger by their lack of reverence for it. They experienced the terrifying power of God's judgment, which in turn caused them to recognize God's holiness: "Who is able to stand before the Lord, this holy God?" (v. 20). Such demonstrations of God's awesome power through his terrible and glorious acts of redemption and judgment always bring God's people to an awareness of his holiness.

A People of Power

Holiness as power. If we are to be holy as God is holy, what implications does this aspect of holiness have for holiness of heart and life among the people of God? *It will mean that God's people will be a people of power.*

God's holiness is manifest in his power. If our holiness is a reflection of God's, then our holiness will be manifest in power too. God's holy people will be a powerful people—not powerful in themselves, not powerful according to the world's standards, but powerful because the power of God is manifest in their lives.

According to Scripture God's power becomes operative in his people through the presence of God's Spirit in their lives. The power of God is manifest in them not because of their own might or power, but because God's Spirit is at work in them (Zech. 4:6). In Old Testament times, however, the Spirit was not given to the whole people of God, but only to select individuals—usually prophets, priests, and kings—for special tasks. So we are told that the Spirit of the Lord came upon Gideon (Judg. 6:34), or Samson (Judg. 14:6) or David (I Sam. 16:13) or Zechariah (II Chron. 24:20) and enabled them to work powerfully for God. Yet the prophet Joel promises there will come a time when the Spirit will be poured out on all God's people—men and women, young and old, slave and free (Joel 2:28-29).

After Christ's resurrection, that promise was fulfilled on the Day of Pentecost when the Holy Spirit was poured out on the believers gathered in the upper room (Acts 2:1-21). And when the Holy Spirit came upon them so did the power of God, just as Jesus had predicted (Acts 1:8). That's why the earliest

Christian community was a community of great power (Acts 4:33). Even those who opposed them acknowledged their power (Acts 4:7). Some even tried to buy it (Acts 8:18-22).

People in that community had power to witness boldly for Christ. What a dramatic contrast between the disciples after the resurrection hiding behind closed doors "for fear of the Jews" (John 20:19), and those same disciples after Pentecost speaking the word of God boldly and unafraid (Acts 4:13, 31). Think of Peter. On the night of Christ's arrest he was afraid to admit he knew Jesus even to a lowly servant-girl (Mark 14:66-72). But after Pentecost he speaks boldly before the Sanhedrin, the supreme council of the Jews (Acts 4:5-22).

Throughout the book of Acts we see the power of the early Christian community in its boldness to witness for Christ. Jesus had promised that when they had received power, they would be his witnesses from Jerusalem to the ends of the earth (Acts 1:8). As the book of Acts unfolds, so does the fulfillment of that promise. They witness boldly in Jerusalem (4:13, 31, 33), in Judea and Samaria (8:4); in Asia Minor (14:3), and in Greece (19:8). The very last verse of the book describes Paul's ministry in Rome. He was "proclaiming the kingdom of God and teaching about the Lord Jesus Christ with all boldness and without hindrance" (28:31). The promise is still unfolding!

The power of the earliest Christian community was also evident in the signs and wonders, the miracles which took place in their midst. Just as Jesus was "attested" by God through the miracles, signs, and wonders which God did through him (2:22), so were the early Christian leaders. "Awe came upon everyone" because of many signs and wonders (2:43). Peter and John healed a crippled beggar (3:1-10). Stephen "did great wonders and signs among the people" (6:8). So did Philip (8:6) and Paul and Barnabas (14:3, 15:12).

The purpose of these signs and wonders is stated in Acts 14:3, where the ministry of Paul and Barnabas in the city of Iconium is described. They spoke boldly for the Lord there, and God "testified to the word of his grace by granting signs and wonders to be done through them." Miracles, signs, and wonders confirmed the power and the truth of the gospel (cf. Heb. 2:4). Such occurrences were not ends in themselves, but were given to convince people that the Christians were of God and that what they were saying about Jesus Christ was true.

It is much easier to explain a reality which everyone acknowledges than it is to defend a theory! When the people saw the man who had been lame from birth "walking and leaping and praising God" (Acts 3:8), they were "all ears" when Peter stood up to explain what had happened. The miracle set the stage for the sermon he preached. Everyone wanted to know how this man had been healed. And when Peter declared he had been healed by the resurrected Christ, the healed man was living, convincing proof that Peter's explanation was true.

The power of the early Christian community was also evident in their willingness to suffer for Christ. On one occasion Peter and John were flogged by the Jewish authorities for their refusal to stop preaching and teaching about Jesus. Their reaction to what happened is incredible: "They rejoiced that they were considered worthy to suffer dishonor for the sake of the name" (Acts 5:41).

Yet this attitude toward suffering was not uncommon among the early Christians. They were willing to make any sacrifice, endure any hardship, face any difficulty for the sake of the gospel. They were even willing to lay their lives on the line—and many of them did. Stephen was stoned to death. James was executed. Paul experienced every kind of suffering imaginable (II Cor. 11:16-33), before he was finally beheaded in Rome. Through their suffering they demonstrated a power which was totally foreign and so appeared foolish to the world—the power of the cross. As Paul expressed it, "We are always being given up to death for

Jesus' sake, so that the life of Jesus may be made visible in our mortal flesh" (II Cor. 4:11).

Turning Away from Worldly Power

It would be easy at this point to bemoan the lack of power in the average United Methodist congregation today. How unlike the early Christian community we are! And how unlike the early Methodists! Those around us are not attracted to us because they see little or no evidence of the power of God working in our midst. But rather than pointing out all the evidence of our impotence, let us consider what we must do to become a people of power like the early Christians.

To begin with, we must repent of our infatuation and obsession with the wrong kind of power—power according to the world's definition of power. We can't be filled with God's power and self-serving, worldly power at the same time. The two are antithetical. In the world's eyes, God's power is sheer foolishness (I Cor. 1:18–2:5). If we are seeking worldly power, we will have no interest in the power of God except to subvert it for our own selfish purposes. We must first turn away from our lusting after worldly, self-serving power before we can open ourselves to the power of God.

How does our infatuation and obsession with self-serving, worldly power manifest itself in our congregations and in our church? It manifests itself in our infatuation with size, status, programs and prestige—measures that the world uses to define power and greatness.

Several years ago, I was working in a small United Methodist church whose members were continually putting themselves down because they were so small. They wished so much they could be like "big churches" that had so much more to offer than they did.

One day I was thinking about their youth program. They

didn't have one to speak of! Yet as I considered the dozen or so young adults who had been nurtured in that church during the past several decades, I thought to myself, "In terms of the quality of Christian discipleship evident in their lives, I would gladly stack them up against any group of young adults who are the product of any large church's high-powered youth program." Growing up in the close-knit, intergenerational fellowship of that small church where they were encouraged and affirmed and where the Christian faith was lived out before them, those young adults had been profoundly formed as Christian disciples.

That congregation had been "successful" according to God's standards. They had imparted genuine Christian faith to their children. But they felt like a failure because they were grasping for greatness and success according to the world's standards. They were seeking the wrong kind of power, when all along the power of God was quietly at work in their midst.

Our infatuation with worldly power is also evident in the way we define the political task of the church. When we watch the evening news on television, we are constantly given the impression that what matters most happens at the level of government and politics. Of course, news reporters never actually say that; but since they spend so much time reporting news related to those things, it is an unquestioned assumption.

Unfortunately, our church has bought in to that assumption. We have allowed the media to define what news is for us. So we think that if we are to be powerful and influential and important, we must be political *as the world defines politics*.

Stanley Hauerwas and William Willimon maintain that both conservative and liberal Christians in America have fallen into this way of thinking. Consequently, although the results of their political strategies may look quite different, their strategies are essentially the same:

Christian politics has therefore come to mean, for both conservative and liberal Christians, Christian social activism. Of course, conservative and liberal Christians may differ on the particulars of just what a truly Christian social agenda looks like, but we are one in our agreement that we should use our democratic power in a responsible way to make the world a better place in which to live.[2]

Of course, much of our social activism is to be commended. Reforming the nation is an important part of the mission of the church. But what motivates much of our activism? When it grows out of our attempt to exert power according to the way the world defines power, the church comes to resemble a political party or a lobby group. It ends up utilizing the same methods and tactics such groups use in trying to effect social change. Then, before long those methods and tactics filter down to the church itself. Annual Conferences become dominated by special-interest groups trying to achieve their particular agenda. Jurisdictional Conferences smack of political conventions with delegations maneuvering with each other to get candidates for bishop elected.

We need to repent, to turn away from these and all our ways of lusting after the wrong kind of power. As long as we are seeking worldly, self-serving power, we will never be open to the power of God.

Turning to the Power of the Holy Spirit

To recover God's power in our church and congregations today we must also open ourselves fully to God's power, the power of the Holy Spirit. Ever since the day of Pentecost when the Holy Spirit was poured out, the church has been living in the age of the Spirit. The Holy Spirit is fully available to us. We can be "filled with the Holy Spirit," just as the early Christians were (Acts 2:4; 4:8, 31; 6:3, 5; 7:55; 9:17; 11:24; 13:9).

Before he ascended to the Father, Jesus commanded his disciples to wait in Jerusalem until they had been "clothed with power from on high" (Luke 24:49). We too need to wait upon God until we have been clothed with power. And when that happens—make no mistake about it—the power of God will manifest itself in our lives and in our congregations just as it did among the earliest Christians. There will be a boldness about our witness for Christ. There will be signs and wonders done in our midst. There will be joyful suffering for the cause of Christ.

We need to seek earnestly the fullness and power of the Holy Spirit. But for many of us this is difficult: as soon as we mention the Holy Spirit thoughts of religious fanaticism, emotionalism, and divisiveness come to mind. We may know someone who "overbelieves" in the Holy Spirit—someone who is impulsive, overbearing, and assumes all his thoughts and impressions are directly from God. We may know of a congregation that was split over controversy about the Holy Spirit. The fire of the Spirit became wildfire; and as a result, many sincere, well-meaning people were burned.

As a result, we are afraid of getting burned. We are afraid of going off the deep end. We don't want to become overbearing fanatics. We don't want to be divisive. And so we go to the other extreme by becoming overly cautious, even fearful of any emphasis on the Holy Spirit. In our efforts to prevent spiritual wildfire, we snuff out the fire itself!

Bishop Richard Wilke points out that as a denomination we have done this more than once:

> I believe that we are even more afraid of the Spirit than we are of the Word. We could not hold the Salvation Army, started by a Methodist preacher. We could not hold the Assemblies of God, started by Methodist preachers. We could not hold the Latin Methodist Pentecostals, started by Methodist missionaries.[3]

In each case, partly because of our fear of fanaticism and spiritual wildfire, these groups were forced out—and an opportunity to channel tremendous amounts of spiritual vitality and creativity into the life of our church was lost. As one United Methodist leader acknowledged to a conference of Nazarene pastors—another group started by Methodists which we couldn't hold: "When you pulled away from us, you took the fire and left us with the stove!"

So we must put away our fear and once again learn to be radically yet responsibly open to the Holy Spirit. To be radically open means we recognize that when the Holy Spirit comes with power, there is generally some untidiness about it. Where there is fire there is smoke too! People can be affected by the Spirit in strange ways. Quakers quake, Shakers shake, Methodists shout (at least they used to!), pentecostals and charismatics are slain in the Spirit. Such things will continue to happen. When the Holy Spirit comes, everything will *not* always be done decently and in order according to our standards of propriety! And although we should not encourage or put a premium on sensational or unusual manifestations of the Spirit, we should not be shocked or afraid when they happen either.

Yet while we are to be radically open to the Holy Spirit, we also are to be *responsibly open*. This means we are not to believe every spirit, but we are to "test the spirits to see whether they are from God" (I John 4:1). We have a responsibility to measure every real or supposed revelation against the touchstone of Scripture. We have a responsibility to see that any extraordinary gift of the Spirit (for example, prophecy, tongues, miracles) is normed and judged by and the ordinary fruit of the Spirit (for example, love, joy, peace, patience). In short, we have a responsibility to keep the fire of the Spirit in the fireplace.

A holy people—holy as God is holy. A people of power—because we have opened ourselves fully to the power of the Holy Spirit. That is what we are called to be. Are we willing to turn away from our own grasping after power and turn to the Holy Spirit so we can be clothed with the power of God?

Notes

1. Otto Kaiser, *Isaiah 1–12* (Philadelphia: Westminster, 1972), p. 78.
2. Stanley Hauerwas and William H. Willimon, *Resident Aliens* (Nashville: Abingdon Press, 1989), p. 37.
3. Richard B. Wilke, *Signs and Wonders* (Nashville: Abingdon Press, 1989), pp. 135-36.

6

Called to Purity

In the last three chapters, we have been thinking about what Isaiah saw when he had his vision of a holy God. He saw God high and exalted. He saw God's glory filling the temple. He saw the awesome power of God. But up to this point, Isaiah himself has been silent. He hasn't uttered a word. In the presence of such an awesome holy God he is awestruck—utterly speechless.

But now it begins to dawn on him what is happening. And we can imagine him thinking to himself, "King Uzziah—all he did was to go into the temple and try to burn some incense. Look what happened to him. He became a wretched leper. But now here I am in the very presence of God himself. What in the world will happen to me?"

Now the futility and hopelessness of his situation begins to sink in. In seeing God, he has seen himself! He can no longer keep silent. In utter desperation he cries out, "Woe is me! I am lost, for I am a man of unclean lips, and I live among a people of unclean lips; yet my eyes have seen the King, the Lord of hosts!" (Isa. 6:5).

Isaiah has heard the seraphs cry out, "Holy, holy, holy." Lepers, when they came within hearing distance of others, were required to cry out, "Unclean! Unclean! Unclean!" Unlike King Uzziah, Isaiah doesn't have the dreaded disease. But

having encountered God, he is painfully aware that he is a leper
—a moral and spiritual leper. Like Uzziah he too has come into
the presence of a holy God when he was totally unfit to do so. In
the presence of a holy God—a God of absolute purity—he sees
his own unholiness, his impurity, as never before.

God's Absolute Purity

When Isaiah finally responds, he does not say, "Woe is
me, I am so small. Look how little I am and how great God
is!" The gulf between God's infiniteness and his finiteness is
not what disturbs him most. Rather, it is the gulf between
God's character and his character. In his vision, Isaiah is
given a glimpse of God's absolute purity, God's moral
perfection, and it completely overwhelms him.

The Scripture says that God is the "Father of lights" (James
1:17) and that God "dwells in unapproachable light" (I Tim.
6:16). When Isaiah caught a glimpse of the absolute purity of
God, his own moral goodness melted away like metal in a
white-hot blast furnace. Here we encounter another aspect of
the holiness of God. God is not only separate from creation, he
is also separate from all sin, evil, and impurity. "God is light
and in him there is no darkness at all" (John 1:5). And when the
pure light of God's holiness shines forth, it exposes everything
that is impure. Like Isaiah, in the presence of God's absolute
purity, we feel unclean and we cry out, "Woe is me!"

Yet God does not leave Isaiah to wallow in his uncleanness,
nor does he leave us. One of the seraphs touches Isaiah's
unclean lips with a live coal from the altar and declares, "Your
guilt has departed and your sin is blotted out" (Isa. 6:7). God,
whose holiness is manifest in his absolute moral purity, not
only is holy in himself, but, as we have stressed before, God
desires to *make* holy. He is the "Holy One" whose "eyes are too
pure to behold evil" and who "cannot look on wrongdoing"
(Hab. 1:12-13). But in the face of evil and wrongdoing, God

does not turn away. Instead God works to purify and make clean. God works to create a people who are holy as he is holy, a people who reflect his absolute purity.

Purity Among God's People

Throughout the Scriptures we see a constant call for purity among the people of God. In the priestly tradition of the Old Testament, that call is primarily concerned with the need for ceremonial or ritual purity among God's people. In the writings of the Old Testament prophets, the call to purity is extended and spiritualized. A holy God, the prophets insist, wants more from his people than outward ceremonial purity. In fact, the Holy One is chiefly concerned about their moral purity. Sacrifices and cleansing rituals will not make people clean as long as they continue their unjust, unethical behavior. They need a cleansing of their actions as well.

Among the prophets the call to moral purity is especially linked with the purity of social justice and equity in human relations. This is the chief means by which the purity required by God's holiness is attained. So the prophets constantly speak out against the people for tolerating injustice and oppression.

The wisdom literature of the Old Testament, particularly some of the Psalms and the book of Job, also stresses moral purity. Here, however, moral purity is more closely linked with personal rather than social ethics. "O Lord, who may abide in your tent? Who may dwell on your holy hill?" asks the writer of Psalm 15. Back comes the answer: those who walk blamelessly (v. 2), who speak truthfully (v. 2), who control their tongue and refrain from gossip (v. 3), who shun evil and fear God (v. 4), who keep their promises (v. 4), and who do not take advantage of the innocent (v. 5).

The book of Job stresses the purity of personal conduct, as Job maintains his innocence in the face of all the accusations of his friends. Job goes even further by calling for purity of inner motive, not just outward compliance to God's norms. Above all, what God desires from his people is purity of heart.

Yet because of their divided loyalties, God's people were largely unable to attain this level of moral purity required by God's holiness. The prophet Ezekiel thus looks to a time when God himself will act "for the sake of my holy name" (Ezek. 36:22) to cleanse his people so they can follow him wholeheartedly:

> I will sprinkle clean water upon you and you shall be clean from all your uncleannesses, and from all your idols I will cleanse you. A new heart I will give you, and a new spirit I will put within you. . . .
> I will put my spirit within you, and make you follow my statutes and be careful to observe my ordinances (Ezek. 36:25-27).

In the New Testament the same call for moral purity is heard. "Blessed are the pure in heart," declares Jesus, "for they will see God" (Matt. 5:8). He carries on a running debate with the Pharisees who are scrupulous about outward ritual purity, but neglect purity of heart (Mark 7:1-23). The writers of the epistles call the Christian communities to turn away from the sensual outlook of the pagans who are "greedy to practice every kind of impurity" (Eph. 4:19). In particular, they are to abstain from all forms of sexual immorality, "for God did not call us to impurity but in holiness" (I Thess. 4:7). In defining "religion that is pure and undefiled" the writer of James echoes this same concern. Pure religion is "to keep oneself unstained by the world." But he couples this with the prophetic emphasis on purity as social justice. Pure religion is "to care for orphans and widows in their distress" (James 1:27).

Purity for Today

The call to purity is clear throughout Scripture. But once again, we ask what this means for our congregations and churches today. To be holy as God is holy calls us to be a people who are pure and undefiled before God, but what particular implications does that have for us? What are the particular areas today where God is calling us to be pure?

From our study of Scripture, there are many areas we could consider. However, we want to simply focus upon one—the need for sexual purity among God's people today. Among the early Christians, surrounded by a sea of immorality in the pagan Greco-Roman world, sexual purity was considered a critical issue, and it has become a critical issue for us in our post-Christian pagan context today.

In many areas the leaders of the early church allowed for diversity of opinion and practice. However, with regard to sexual immorality in all its forms, they left no room for diversity among believers. Sexual purity was a non-negotiable demand laid upon everyone who desired to be a Christian. William Barclay helps us understand how revolutionary this demand was in their day.

It is the simple truth that Christianity brought into the world a new idea of sexual purity. The ancient world attached little stigma to sexual relationships either before or outside marriage. They were indeed customary and the accepted practice. In the period which is the immediate background of the New Testament, Seneca could say that there were Roman women who were married to be divorced and divorced to be married, and who distinguished the years, not by the names of the consuls but by the names of their husbands (Seneca, *On Benefits*, 3.16.1-3). 'Innocence,' he says, 'is not rare; it is non-existent' (*On Anger*, 2.8). . . . Juvenal tells how Messalina, the Empress wife of Claudius, used to slip out of the royal palace at nights and go down to serve in the common brothels. She was ever the last to leave, and would return to the imperial pillow with all the odors of the stews (Juvenal, *Satires*, 6.114-132).

As for homosexuality, it was what Dollinger called 'the great national disease of Greece' (*The Gentile and the Jew*, ii. 239). J. J. Chapman says that it had become 'racial, indigenous, and ingrown like a loathsome fungus spreading steadily through a forest' (*Lucian, Plato and Greek Morals*, 132, 133). Into a world of sexual anarchy Christianity came with this new demand for absolute and uncompromising purity, insisting that a man must keep himself 'unstained from the world' (James 1:27).[1]

We have quoted this passage at length because it underscores the radical nature of the Christian call to sexual purity in contrast to the first-century pagan context and because its vivid description of that context also describes our world today!

There was a time in America when Christian standards of sexual morality had a profound influence on public behavior—even in the film industry. For example, in 1934 the production code of the Motion Picture Producers and Distributors of America listed these strictures:

—The sanctity of the institution of marriage and the home shall be upheld. Pictures shall not infer that low forms of sex relationships are the accepted or common thing.
—Excessive and lustful kissing, lustful embracing, suggestive postures and gestures, are not to be shown.
—Pointed profanity (this includes the words God, Lord, Jesus Christ—unless used reverently—Hell, S.O.B., damn, Gawd), or other profane and vulgar expressions, however used, is forbidden.
—Ministers of religion . . . should not be used as comic characters or as villains.[2]

Until the advent of the sexual revolution in the 1960s, only a few producers resisted this code. Now almost all would call it utterly ridiculous. In fact in motion pictures today, almost the exact opposite of each of the restrictions listed above has become the norm!

With regard to sexual attitudes and practices, we are living in a pagan, post-Christian society today. Premarital, extramarital, and postmarital sex; living together before marriage; infidelity; and homosexual practices are common and accepted. More or less anything goes between consenting adults. Sexual attitudes and practices have been disconnected from morality and are now considered a matter of personal preference. People are encouraged to choose from a smorgasbord of morally equivalent sexual life-styles the one or ones that seem right for them. What matters most is to be true to oneself. So "Intelligent Choice of Sexual Lifestyle," a California sex education curriculum, advises seventh graders to set a "purely personal standard of sexual behavior."[3]

How have we as a church and as congregations responded to all this? Have we been a voice crying in this sexual wilderness, calling people to biblical standards of morality? Have we been like the early Christians, clear and uncompromising in our call to sexual purity?

The tragedy is that within our church itself there are those calling for the acceptance of the very sexual practices and life-styles which the Scripture clearly condemns. Why else has every General Conference of The United Methodist Church since 1972 debated legislation that would change the church's position that homosexual practice is incompatible with Christian teaching?

In his message to the church at Thyatira, the risen Christ declares: "But I have this against you: you tolerate that woman Jezebel, who calls herself a prophet and is teaching and beguiling my servants to practice fornication" (Rev. 2:20). He has the same thing against our church today! It is time for us to clearly and uncompromisingly affirm biblical standards of sexual purity and to stop tolerating the constant belittling, undermining, and challenging of those standards which has been going on in our church.

This does not mean we have to deal harshly or judgmentally with those who fall short of those standards. We need to be compassionate and forgiving with those who have fallen into sexual sin, especially in this day and age when we are confronted so often with sexual temptation. Sexual habits and behavior patterns are difficult to break. We must be patient and understanding with people as they seek to change. At the same time, we must continue to set forth biblical standards of sexual purity as God's will and intention for us all.

Those standards may seem high, even unrealistic in the day in which we live. They seemed high in the first century as well. But the early church did not hesitate to call people to those standards because it believed that the gospel provided the power to live up to them.

In writing to the Christians in the decadent, sex-saturated city of Corinth, Paul leaves no doubt about the Christian standard for sexual purity: "Do not be deceived! Fornicators, idolaters, adulterers, male prostitutes, sodomites, thieves, the greedy, drunkards, revilers, robbers—none of these will inherit the kingdom of God" (I Cor. 6:10). But Paul is not naive, out of touch with their present sexual temptations or their past sexual history. "And this is what some of you used to be," he adds. He faces the reality of their situation head on. Then he reminds them of the transforming power of the gospel: "But you were washed, you were sanctified, you were justified in the name of the Lord Jesus Christ and in the Spirit of our God" (v. 11). The gospel has the power to cleanse us from the sexual sins of our past, and the power to keep us sexually pure in the present and future.

Perhaps our tendency to tolerate sexual impurity in the church today and our hesitancy to call people to clear biblical standards is a reflection of our loss of confidence in the power of the gospel. We are giving in to pressure from without because there has been an erosion of confidence within. We simply do not believe enough in the cleansing and keeping power of the gospel, nor do we expect to see that power demonstrated in our midst.

God's holiness is manifest in his absolute purity. God calls us to be pure. Through his Spirit he can make us pure. If we are willing, God can cleanse us from all our impurities and cause us to follow him wholeheartedly (Ezek. 36:25-27). Will we hear his call to purity? Will we receive his grace which can make us and keep us pure? Will we be holy as God is holy?

Notes

1. William Barclay, *Turning to God* (London: Epworth Press, 1964), p. 66.
2. "Biblical Morality and Motion Pictures," *People of Destiny* (Nov./Dec. 1986), p. 25.
3. Quoted in Charles Colson, *Against the Night* (Ann Arbor: Servant Books, 1989), p. 81.

7

Abounding in Love

Isaiah's desperate cry, "I am a man of unclean lips," is answered by God's action and declaration through the seraph, "Now that this has touched your lips, your guilt has departed and your sin is blotted out" (Isa. 6:7). As a result, Isaiah's "Woe is me!" is transformed into "Here am I! Send me."

God's Self-giving Love

Here then is a fifth and final aspect of the holiness of God: God's holiness is manifest in God's self-giving love. God does not simply leave Isaiah with new awareness of his impurity. His holiness issues in sympathy, not apathy. God redeems the situation. God is concerned about Isaiah's well-being, so he acts to take away Isaiah's uncleanness and bestow upon him new mission and a purpose. God's holiness issues in his love.

Yet many people do not associate holiness and love with each other. Sometimes the two have even been set against each other. As Joseph Cooke says, "Many of us have been taught that holiness and love are somehow opposed to each other—as if holiness were at one extreme of God's nature and love at the other, and holiness would blot us out if love couldn't find a way to prevent it."[1] The truth, however, is just the opposite. Rather than being opposed to it, God's self-giving love is rooted in God's holiness. It is, in fact, its supreme manifestation.

In his discussion of the holiness of God, theologian Karl Barth emphasizes this point. There is no doubt, he says, that the holiness of God means that God is exalted over his people, Israel, and separate from them. But it means this "only because it means primarily and decisively this—that God has adopted and chosen Israel as His child, has given it His promise, and has already conferred upon it His gracious help."[2] Barth then goes on to point out the number of Old Testament passages where God's holiness and God's self-giving love are linked together, passages where *because* of his redemptive love God is called holy. For example, Moses' exultation, "Who is like you, majestic in holiness" (Exod. 15:11), is prompted by God's deliverance of his people at the Red Sea. Hannah's joyous declaration, "There is no Holy One like the Lord" (I Sam. 2:2), follows the birth of Samuel, which was an answer to Hannah's prayer that God would allow her to conceive. And the Psalmist's affirmation, "Your way, O God, is holy" (77:13), is made while reciting God's gracious acts on behalf of Israel. So Barth concludes, "Holy means separate, that which confronts, arousing awe and the sense of obligation. But it clearly means primarily and fundamentally that which singles out, blesses, helps and restores, and only in this positive connection does it have that other significance."[3]

So God's holiness and God's love should not be set over against each other. The two are intimately bound up together, so much so that God's acts of redemptive, self-giving love are the most sure and certain proof that God is holy. God is holy *because* he reaches out in redemptive, self-giving love.

A People Who Love

To be holy as God is holy—what does that mean for our congregations in relation to this aspect of holiness? *We must be a people who reach out toward others with self-giving, redemptive love.* God has reached out to us with such love. We in turn must reach out to others. Our holiness is to be measured by our love.

The apostle Paul seems to have this in mind when he prays for the congregation at Thessalonica:

> And may the Lord make you increase and abound in love for one another and for all, just as we abound in love for you. And may he so strengthen your hearts in holiness that you may be blameless before our God and Father at the coming of our Lord Jesus with all his saints. (I Thess. 3:12-13)

Notice the close connection here between holiness and love. Abounding in love for one another and being strengthened in holiness go together. The exhortation in Hebrews 12:14 is similar: "Pursue peace with everyone, and the holiness without which no one will see the Lord."

Notice too in the prayer for the Thessalonians, Paul delineates the two major spheres where we are to love. We are to abound in love "for one another" and "for all." Love for one another has to do with the love Christians express for other Christians, other members of the body of Christ. We are to abound in love in the sphere of the church. Love for all is the love Christians express toward those outside the fellowship of the church. We are to abound in love in the sphere of the world.

As congregations, then, how well is our holiness expressed in our love for one another and for all? We may talk much about love, but is it taking concrete shape in our actions? Do people "know we are Christians by our love"?

Sometimes churches and congregations can talk much about the need for love. We can sing about it, but to those around us, both in and outside the church, we fail to communicate love. The call to holiness is a call to love. So let's consider the measure of our love first for one another, and then for all.

Love for One Another

Christ "loved the church and gave himself up for her" (Eph. 5:25). He sacrificed himself even to the point of death. In the same way, we are to love other members of the body of Christ. Such sacrificial love for each other characterized the early Christian community. They gave themselves to one another, even to the point of selling their possessions so that the needs of the whole community were met (Acts 2:44).

They loved each other the way brothers and sisters, members of the same family love each other (Rom. 12:10, I Thess. 4:9; Heb. 13:1-3; I Peter 1:22-23). Growing out of their sense of being God's family, they were drawn together into a close-knit fellowship which transcended barriers of race, sex, class, and education.

In his in-depth study of evangelism in the early church, Michael Green points out that this characteristic—their familial love for one another despite all their differences— gave the early church its drawing power. "Here were societies in which aristocrats and slaves, Roman citizens and provincials, rich and poor mixed on equal terms and without distinction: societies which possessed a quality of caring and love which was unique. Herein lay its attraction."[4]

What about our congregations today? Does our sacrificial love for one another, our unity amid all our differences, convince the world around us of the reality of God in our midst? In *Habits of the Heart*, Robert Bellah shows how an unhealthy individualism has infected all American culture— including our religion.[5] When we come to church, we bring our "what's in it for me" and our "if you don't meet my needs I'll go somewhere else" attitudes with us. What a challenge

74

for our congregations today—to stand against the prevailing attitudes of our culture by showing sacrificial love for one another, by putting the unity of the family of God above our own desires and wants! And what an opportunity—to demonstrate by our distinctiveness the reality of God in our midst! Then newcomers will say, "There's only one way to explain their love and commitment to one another: God is alive and working here."

Love for All

As a holy people we are to abound in love for one another, but our love must not stop there. It must overflow the boundaries of our congregations to encompass everyone. God loves the world. God gave himself for the world—not just the church. So should we.

In reaching out in love to those outside the fellowship of the church, we are naturally drawn to people we are comfortable with, people who are like ourselves. Certainly we should begin with them. Do we have family members, relatives, friends, co-workers, business associates, who are outside of Christ and the fellowship of the church? We are to abound in self-giving, sacrificial love toward them.

But our love must extend beyond them. The "all" we are to love also includes the people who are unlike us, those with whom we are uncomfortable. Since they are the people we often overlook, let's consider the love our congregations should express toward them.

Every community has social outcasts, forgotten people, people who are looked down upon. Robert Webber and Rodney Clapp call them "parenthetical people."[6] They are the persons society puts in parentheses, making them optional, dispensable, and unimportant. We tend to avoid these people whenever we can, so very few of them are ever found in our congregations. They are not the kind of persons we seek out when we are looking for church members. Yet as a holy people who are called to love all, shouldn't our love encompass them too?

Think of how Jesus reached out to the "parenthetical people" of his day. Instead of putting them in parentheses, Jesus put exclamation points after them to stress how important they were to him. He dined with social outcasts—tax collectors, prostitutes, and sinners. Rather than causing him to withdraw, his holiness drew him toward them. Jesus touched lepers. He felt compassion for widows. He fellowshiped with the poor and called them blessed. In a day when women were considered stupid and looked upon as little more than property, Jesus conversed with them and treated them with dignity and respect. Like women, children were ignored in his day. Yet Jesus said, "Let the little children come to me" (Mark 10:14), and exhorted his followers to become childlike in spirit. Jesus' love and compassion for the marginalized people of his time—the outcasts, the poor, women, and children—was one of the most remarkable aspects of his ministry.

To abound in love for all means that we too, as individuals and congregations, reach out to the forgotten people, the parenthetical people of our communities. Like Jesus we ought to have a special place in our heart for them. We should be standing in solidarity with them—bearing their pain and working for justice on their behalf.

Here is how change began to happen in one United Methodist congregation of about three hundred members located in a small rural town. One day the pastor of the church was sitting in his study reading a book on evangelism. The book described the evangelistic strategy of Jesus—how he seemed to target people who were considered outcasts in his day.

The pastor put down the book and began to apply what he was reading to himself and his congregation: "That means that if Jesus were living today, and he came to our town, he would probably spend a good deal of time with the people we consider outcasts. But I wonder, who would those people be? Who are the outcasts of our town?"

As he pondered his own question, two groups of people came to mind. There was a home for semi-retarded and older adults on one end of town. He had often referred to it as a "home for throw-away people." For the most part, the residents there were not so mentally retarded or physically incapacitated that they had to be institutionalized. They were just people nobody wanted, so they had been sent there to live either by their families or the state. Most of them were not confined to the home. They were free to walk around town. Often people would encounter them on the streets or in the local grocery store. They were friendly and didn't create any problems in the community. But often they were the brunt of people's jokes. Almost everyone laughed at them and made fun of them behind their backs.

Then he began to think about another group of people— the "druggies" as they were called—those in their late teens and early twenties, who were regular drug users. They were loud, boisterous, dirty, and unkempt. Some were unemployed and were stealing to support their drug habit. The people in that conservative, established little town looked on them with contempt. They were the scum of the community. Everyone wished they would leave and never come back.

Then the pastor thought, "If Jesus came to our town, I'll bet he'd spend a lot of time with those people. They are the outcasts of this community." But then he had another thought: "Jesus is here in our town! After all, isn't our church an expression of his body? Aren't we his hands and his feet? And if that's the case, shouldn't we be doing what he would be doing if he were physically present in our community? Shouldn't we be spending time with the same kind of people he would spend time with if he were actually here?"

Several weeks later in a sermon, the pastor challenged the congregation. "If we are the body of Christ," he said, "we should be doing the things Jesus would do if he were here. When he was on earth, he reached out in love to the outcasts, to those who were considered worthless and insignificant. If he were here in our community, wouldn't he do the same?"

Then he spoke to the congregation about the two groups of people who were the outcasts of that community—the residents of the home and the "druggies." You could hear a pin drop in the sanctuary as he was describing them. "There may be other outcasts among us," he said, "but these two groups are a good place to start. If our church is going to be faithful to Jesus, I believe we need to be spending time with these people. We need to be involved in ministry to them."

He closed his sermon by issuing a challenge: "If any of you can think of some concrete practical ways we can begin ministering to these people, get in touch with me. Let's talk. Let's see what we can come up with as we ask the Lord to show us how our congregation can minister to the outcasts of our community."

After the service, a middle-aged woman approached the pastor. "I've been concerned about the people in that home too," she said. "I have a couple of afternoons a week when I don't have to work. I have also done some craft programs with older adults. I would be willing to go to that home once a week on one of my free afternoons and work with the residents who are interested in working with crafts."

"Go to it," the pastor said. "We'll try to get some others to assist you and help pay for the materials." In two weeks the program was started. The residents were thrilled. It wasn't much, but no one was doing anything like that for them. Most of all they felt that somebody cared. It wasn't long before some of them began attending worship on Sunday.

Later that week two young couples dropped by the pastor's office. "We've been concerned about the druggies for a long time," they said. "We were there once ourselves, and Jesus delivered us. They need to know he can do the same for them. Remember the coffee houses that were popular a few years ago? We were wondering if we could start something like that in the church basement on Friday nights. These kids need a place where they can come and unwind. They need people who will accept them and listen to them. They need to know that there's hope in Christ." Some of the members of the church were reluctant, but it wasn't long before that ministry was under way, too.

So that's what happened in one congregation that simply asked, "Who are the parenthetical people, the outcasts of our community?" Then they began taking some concrete steps to reach out to those people in love.

What would happen if your congregation did the same thing?

Notes

1. Joseph Cooke, "Holy, Holy, Holy: God's Most Misunderstood Attribute," *Eternity* 30 (March 1979), p. 22.
2. Karl Barth, *Church Dogmatics,* II/1 (Edinburgh: T. & T. Clark, 1956), pp. 360-61.
3. Ibid., p. 361.
4. Michael Green, *Evangelism in the Early Church* (Grand Rapids: William B. Eerdmans Publishing Co., 1970), p. 182.
5. Robert Bellah, *Habits of the Heart* (New York: Harper & Row, 1985).
6. Robert Webber and Rodney Clapp, *People of the Truth* (New York: Harper & Row, 1988), p. 45.

8

Experiencing God's Gracious Touch

Isaiah had a vision of the holiness of God. If we, the people called United Methodist, are to recover a passion for holiness of heart and life, we too, like Isaiah, need to catch a fresh vision of God's holiness. In the last five chapters we have been thinking about this second key ingredient in the transformation of an unholy people to a holy people. We have been focusing on Isaiah's vision and what it means for us today. Now in this chapter we move on to consider a third necessary ingredient if there is to be a renewal of holiness among us; *we need an experience of God's gracious touch on our lives.* Lacking that, our awareness of our own helplessness and our vision of God's holiness will only drive us to despair. Like Isaiah, we will cry out, "Woe is me, I am doomed." We will have gained a proper understanding of ourselves and a proper understanding of God. But in themselves, those things, as indispensable as they are, will not bring about the transformation we need.

Only an act of God, a divine touch upon our lives, can make that possible. Like Isaiah, we need the seraph to come and touch our lips and declare, "Your guilt has departed and your sin is blotted out" (Isa. 6:7). God must act to cleanse and heal and transform.

In his earnest pursuit of holiness, John Wesley had to learn this lesson the hard way. He had begun seeking holiness in 1725 at the age of twenty-two while he was a master's student at Oxford.

Because of his passion for holiness, in 1729 Wesley joined the small group at Oxford which his brother, Charles, had started. The Holy Club, as they soon came to be called by the students at the university, was a group that gathered daily for study and prayer. The members pledged to be regular in private devotions, to take Communion at least once a week, to carefully watch over their moral conduct, and to visit local prisons once or twice a week. They also agreed to meet with the group each evening from six to nine o'clock for Bible study and discussion of other religious books. Because of the extremely methodical way the group was engaged in the pursuit of holiness, they were nicknamed "Methodists."

Like Isaiah, Wesley had been captured by a vision of holiness. It was that vision which prompted him to volunteer in 1735 for missionary service in Georgia. The experience, as we saw earlier, turned into a fiasco, but good came out of it. As a result of his failure as a missionary, Wesley came to an awareness of his own helplessness. He had been trying to achieve holiness through his own efforts. He now saw the utter futility of that approach. Like Isaiah, he could only cry out, "Woe is me!"

Now the first two ingredients necessary for the renewal of holiness were both present in his life. He had a vision of God's holiness and a vision of his own helplessness. He had seen God and he had seen himself. But where did that leave him? In total despair.

When he returned to England from Georgia in January, 1738, Wesley was confused and desperate—caught between his awareness of the demand to be holy as God is holy, and a growing sense of his own inability to live up to that demand.

Like Isaiah, Wesley needed a touch from God to break out of the vicious cycle he was in; and like Isaiah, that was exactly what he got! Through the influence of Peter Bohler, a Moravian, he soon came to understand that he had been building holiness on the wrong foundation. All his efforts to be holy had been ineffectual because he had been trusting in his own self-effort instead of trusting in the Savior, Jesus Christ. That was why his religion had become so burdensome. His relationship with God was based on his own righteousness, not the righteousness of Christ. He was living under law, not grace.

What he lacked was saving faith, personal trust, and reliance on Christ. But because he lacked it, Wesley concluded that he ought to stop preaching. "No," said Bohler. "Preach faith until you have it; and then, because you have it, you will preach faith." Wesley took his paradoxical advice and it worked. On the evening of May 24, 1738—the day Methodists around the world celebrate as Aldersgate Day—it happened: God touched him.

Earlier that day he had written a friend describing his dilemma:

> I see that the whole law of God is holy, righteous, and good. I know every thought, every temper of my soul ought to bear God's image and superscription. But how am I fallen from the glory of God! I feel that 'I am sold under sin.' . . . God is holy; I am unholy. God is a consuming fire; I am altogether a sinner, meet to be consumed.[1]

How much like Isaiah's "Woe is me"! How painfully aware Wesley was of God's holiness and his own unholiness! But then, like Isaiah, the seraph came and touched his lips. As he describes it in his well-known words:

> In the evening I went very unwillingly to a society in Aldersgate Street, where one was reading Luther's preface of the Epistle to the Romans. About a quarter before nine, while he was describing the change which God works in the heart through faith in Christ, I felt my heart strangely warmed. I felt I did trust in Christ, Christ alone, for salvation; and an assurance was given me that He had taken away my sins, even mine, and saved me from the law of sin and death.[2]

At that moment, Wesley experienced God's gracious touch. He was given saving faith and an assurance of forgiveness, and his life was different. The call to holiness had not changed. He continued to earnestly strive after it as he had since 1725. But now it was holiness which flowed out of faith, not self-effort. It was holiness whose mainspring was Christ himself living in him through faith. It was holiness through the Spirit of holiness, the Holy Spirit, bearing fruit in his life.

Throughout the rest of his life and ministry, Wesley never eased up on the demand to strive after holiness. But after Aldersgate it was not holiness by itself; it was faith leading to holiness. It was holiness set in motion by the touch of God, holiness driven by the Holy Spirit, not the human spirit. Only God's gracious touch provides the dynamic equal to the demand of holiness.

God's touch also fills the life of holiness with happiness and joy. Contrary to what we are so prone to think, the life of holiness is not a life of gloom and doom. Holiness leads to happiness. Isaiah emphasizes this point in his description of a time when God's people will travel upon a highway of holiness: "A highway shall be there, and it shall be called the Holy Way; the unclean shall not travel on it, but it shall be for God's people" (Isa. 35:8). But what will it be like to travel that highway? Will it be a somber, burdensome experience? Just the opposite: "And the ransomed of the Lord shall return, and come to Zion with singing; everlasting joy shall be upon their heads; they shall obtain joy and gladness, and sorrow and sighing will flee away" (Isa. 35:10). Holiness leads to happiness. As we travel along the highway of holiness, sorrow and sighing will flee away.

Isaiah emphasizes this. So does Wesley. In an age that was obsessed with happiness, he said it again and again: only the holy can ever be truly happy. According to Albert Outler, in no less than thirty of his sermons, he rings the changes on this theme.[3]

But it is only the touch of God that fills holiness with happiness. Without God's gracious action in our lives, striving for holiness becomes a heavy burden, an exhausting chore. In describing his pursuit of holiness prior to Aldersgate, Wesley says, "I dragged on heavily."[4] The pursuit of holiness will only weigh us down and wear us out until we experience God's gracious touch. Then it becomes a pursuit filled with joy and delight as we are carried along, not by our own self-effort, but by the dynamic of God's spirit working in us.

God's gracious touch also causes the life of holiness to become other-oriented rather than self-oriented. In describing the difference the experience at Aldersgate made in Wesley's life, Ruppert Davies, the British Methodist scholar, says:

> Until now his immense spiritual and mental energies had been most directly upon himself; he had spent innumerable hours, not only during the preceding months, but for most of his life, brooding upon the state of his soul and trying to improve it. Now those energies were released, and immediately directed outward to those of his fellowmen who stood in need of the same liberation as he himself received. Personal salvation for himself was no longer his all-absorbing aim. In fact, he virtually forgot it in his enterprise to bring salvation to others.[5]

In the next chapter, we will show how a passion for holiness always leads to mission. The pursuit of holiness moves us beyond ourselves to the world God loves. Here we want to stress that without the touch of God that movement toward others will never occur. We will cry, "Woe is me!" as we gain a vision of a holy God coupled with an awareness of our own unholiness. But we will never exclaim, "Here am I; send me!" until we have experienced God's gracious touch upon our lives.

Waiting for God

If there is to be a renewal of holiness of heart and life among the people called United Methodist, both as individuals and congregations we must experience a fresh touch from God. Following his resurrection, Jesus told his disciples to tarry in Jerusalem until they were endued with power from on high. We too must tarry. We must wait for God until he comes and touches us.

We must wait desperately. We are desperate because unless God comes and touches us, we have no hope. All the human effort we can muster will not bring about the renewal we need. Only the Holy One can make us holy. So we need to acknowledge our utter helplessness and our total dependence on God. We need to stop depending on our own efforts and start depending on God.

We must also wait with determination. Jacob said to the angel after he had wrestled with him all night, "I will not let you go until you bless me" (Gen. 32:26). We too need to hold on until God's blessing comes. Sometimes it comes quickly, but more often after a period of time. So we need to be patient and persistent in our waiting for God. We need to keep asking and seeking and knocking until we receive God's gracious life-giving touch.

Finally, we must wait expectantly. We know that we have a Father in heaven who wants to give good gifts to his children (Matt. 7:11). He has promised that if we ask we will receive, if we seek we will find, if we knock the door will be opened (Matt. 7:7-8). So we should approach God boldly and confidently, knowing that we do not have to overcome his reluctance to come to us. We simply need to take hold of his willingness.

We can wait in many different ways, but above all we need to wait through prayer. As the disciples waited to be endued with power they "were constantly devoting themselves to prayer"

(Acts 1:14). We too need to be about the serious business of prayer. Our bishops should call us to specific times of prayer for the renewal of our denomination as a whole. Our pastors should call us to specific times of prayer for the renewal of our congregations. We as individuals should pray regularly for personal renewal and the renewal of our churches.

If we, as God's people, will humble ourselves and pray and seek God's face, then he will cleanse and restore and heal (II Chron. 7:14). Then God will touch us and cause us to seek holiness again.

Notes

1. *Works*, 1, p. 103.
2. *Letters*, I, p. 245.
3. Albert Outler, ed., *The Works of John Wesley*, vol. 1 (Nashville: Abingdon Press, 1984), p. 35.
4. *Works*, 1, p. 100.
5. Ruppert Davies, *Methodism* (London: Epworth Press, 1976), p. 52.

9

Here Am I—
Send Me!

Isaiah has seen the Lord high and lifted up. Through the seraph he has experienced the Lord's cleansing touch upon his lips. But until now he has not heard God speak. The seraphs have spoken—"Holy, holy, holy." Isaiah has spoken—"Woe is me." But God has been silent.

Now God's silence is broken: "Then I heard the voice of the Lord saying, 'Whom shall I send, and who will go for us?' " (Isa. 6:8). Yet when God finally speaks, he doesn't speak directly to Isaiah. When God first spoke to Moses out of the burning bush, God called him by name: "Moses, Moses" (Exod. 3:4). And Moses said, "Here I am." Not so with Isaiah. In fact, we wonder if God is addressing Isaiah at all. God asks, "Who will go for us?" But who is the "us"? Most likely it is the seraphs and the other celestial beings gathered around the heavenly throne. God is asking them, not Isaiah, "Who will go for us?" Isaiah is just an outside observer listening in on their interaction.

But how does Isaiah react when he hears God's question? Immediately he speaks up and volunteers, "Here am I; send me!" He can't keep quiet. For he has seen the dreadful chasm between God's awesome holiness and his own awful uncleanness; and he has also experienced God's miraculous bridging of that chasm. As a result, Isaiah is so overwhelmed with gratitude that he can't help responding to God's question even though he hasn't been asked: "How about me, God? I'll go."

In the face of who God is and who Isaiah is and what God has done, Isaiah can't keep quiet. He wants to serve. Even when God does speak directly to Isaiah, warning him that his message will be rejected by the vast majority of people, he still wants to go.

Isaiah's vision of holiness issues in a call to mission. This is the fourth and final ingredient necessary for the renewal of holiness of heart and life among us. First, a posture of humility. Second, a vision of a holy God. Third, an experience of God's gracious touch. Now fourth, a readiness to respond to God's call to mission in the world. As in the case of Isaiah, this response ought to flow naturally and automatically. God has come and transformed our desperate situation. How can we not be filled with gratitude? How can we not tell others who are desperate what God can do for them?

This fourth ingredient for a revival of holiness flows out of the other three. In fact, it is the fulfillment and culmination of them. Since it can't stand on its own, we don't begin with the call to mission in our efforts to bring about a renewal of holiness. But its absence is a good indication that the other three ingredients are lacking too.

As in the case of Isaiah, the revival of holiness among the early Methodists issued in a movement outward. Their passion for holiness was not only a passion to be holy themselves, but to *spread* scriptural holiness across the land. An authentic revival of holiness inevitably brings with it a revival of mission.

The World Is My Parish

Again, John Wesley's life illustrates the connection between holiness and mission. Even before his Aldersgate experience he understood the connection. As a member of the Holy Club he was busily engaged in preaching, visiting those who were sick or in prison, caring for the poor, witnessing to others about Christ. He even went to serve as a missionary in Georgia.

But for all his diligence and effort, until Aldersgate his ministry was barren and fruitless. First he had to experience God's grace in his own life before he could offer that grace effectively to others. The touch of God transformed Wesley's approach to mission because it transformed him. As Albert Outler says, it changed him "from a harsh zealot of God's judgment to a winsome witness to God's grace, from a censorious critic to an effective pastor, from arrogance to humility."[1]

The clearest indication of this transformation was Wesley's embarrassing descent into field preaching on April 2, 1739, about ten months after Aldersgate. Here is how he records the event in his journal:

> Mon. 2.—At four in the afternoon I submitted to be more vile and proclaimed in the highways the glad tidings of salvation, speaking from a little eminence in the ground adjoining to the city to about three thousand people. The scripture on which I spoke was this, . . . "The Spirit of the Lord is upon me, because he hath anointed me to preach the gospel to the poor. He hath sent me to heal the broken-hearted; to preach deliverance to the captives, and recovery of sight to the blind: To set at liberty them that are bruised, to proclaim the acceptable year of the Lord."[2]

What a shattering, humbling experience for the respectable Oxford don who had been so strict about doing all things decently and in order! Considering the person he was, the fact that he "consented to be more vile" by field preaching was nothing short of a miracle. Wesley was finicky about his personal appearance. He always dressed as neat as a pin, and wouldn't tolerate the slightest speck of dirt on his clothing. He hated commotion and disturbance. He preferred the quiet of a university library or a pastor's study to the noise of a large crowd. Only an experience of God's gracious touch could transform this prim and proper, private little man into a missioner to the common people.

But this is what a renewal of holiness of heart and life always does. It thrusts us out of ourselves and our inhibitions toward people. Like Isaiah, we find ourselves volunteering before we've even been asked: "Here am I. Send me!" A passion for holiness always leads to an urgency to be about God's mission in the world.

The remarkable success of Wesley's initial ventures into field preaching first convinced him that they should be extended to all of England. And so for the next fifty years that is what he did—traveling some 225,000 miles by horseback, preaching 40,000 sermons, winning perhaps as many as 144,000 converts to Christ, establishing a vast network of "classes" and "societies," working tirelessly to spread scriptural holiness across the land. Yet Wesley never became fully comfortable with field preaching. As late as 1772 he confided, "To this day field preaching is a cross to me."[3] But he knew of no better way to reach people with the gospel, so he kept at it.

He was often criticized for engaging in this unconventional form of open-air evangelism even by those who were closest to him. His elder brother Samuel wrote to their mother Susanna, insisting that he would much rather see his brothers John and Charles "picking straws within the walls than preaching in the area of Moorfields."[4] Wesley was also criticized because he would not respect the established boundaries of parishes. He was determined that no ecclesiastical barrier would prevent him from doing his plain duty in offering Christ to others. In his well-known letter to James Harvey he explains why he invades the parishes of other clergy:

> Man forbids me to do this in another's parish: that is, in effect, to do it at all; seeing I have now no parish of my own, nor probably ever shall. Whom, then, shall I hear, God or man? . . .
>
> Suffer me now to tell you my principles in this matter. I look upon all the world as my parish; thus far I mean, that in whatever part of it

I am I judge it meet, right and my bounden duty to declare, unto all that are willing to hear, the glad tidings of salvation.[5]

Because holiness was Wesley's passion, the world was his parish. Contrary to what some taught, Wesley was convinced that Jesus' Great Commission to "Go and make disciples of all nations" (Matt. 2:19-20) was not only addressed to the original apostles. It was intended for all Christians at all times. He was therefore determined to be engaged in that task, and he insisted that every Methodist was too. As he instructed his growing company of lay preachers:

You have nothing to do but save souls. Therefore spend and be spent in this work. . . . Observe: It is not your business to preach so many times, and to take care of this or that society; but to save as many souls as you can; to bring as many sinners as you possibly can to repentance and with all your power to build them up in that holiness without which they cannot see the Lord.[6]

The incredible growth and the spread of Methodism, first in England and then in North America, proves that the early Methodists followed Wesley's instructions. Holiness of heart and life and spreading holiness across the land went hand in hand. By 1844, just sixty years after Methodism had been officially established, it had become the largest Protestant body in the United States. One out of every nineteen Americans was a Methodist. As the national population grew, the church continued to grow too. In 1948 the ratio of Methodists to the total U.S. population had increased to one out of sixteen.

Our Loss of Mission

By 1988, however, just forty years later, that ratio had dropped to one out of twenty-five—a decrease of almost 40 percent. Because our involvement in mission has waned, we have been declining.

In 1988, over 40 percent of all United Methodist congregations received no new persons by Profession of Faith. More than 15,000 congregations received no one—not even one of their own children through confirmation. Included in that group are 130 of the several hundred churches in United Methodism with a thousand or more members. They take care of their own members, and they welcome transfers, but they are obviously not taking seriously the commission to make new disciples.

With regard to new church extension, it was common during the nineteenth century for the Methodist Episcopal Church to average starting one new church a day, and sometimes even two a day. In the 1970s, however, our rate had dwindled to two a month. Now that has increased slightly to four a month, but still it is appallingly low. It is less than one tenth the current rate of new church extension among Southern Baptists. Thus, according to church growth specialist George Hunter, "We are probably starting fewer new congregations today than any other major denomination in the Western hemisphere."[7]

The number of overseas missionaries sent out by our church has also declined drastically in the past few decades—from 1650 in 1968, to 938 in 1980, to 443 in 1988.[8] In 1988 the ratio of missionaries to total denominational membership was one missionary for every 20,268 members. When we compare that ratio with the Southern Baptists whose ratio is 1/3835 or the Disciples of Christ whose ratio is 1/9969, we realize how much we are lacking in concern for world evangelization.

The sad truth is that the majority of United Methodist congregations have substituted meetings, maintenance, methods, and machinery for mission. All these things which are to be the means to our mission—spreading holiness across the land—have become ends in themselves. As a result, instead of fishers of men and women, we have become keepers of the aquarium. Instead of the world being our parish, our parish has become our world. Instead of rewarding clergy who are leaders, we reward those who are managers. We know how to take care of our own flock, but we are blithely indifferent to the lost sheep all around us. We are a church out of focus—a church turned inward upon ourselves, instead of a church turned outward to the world which God loves.

Turning Toward the World

Most of us don't realize how ingrown we have become. We have become so preoccupied with ourselves and our own congregational and denominational concerns that we are blind to the gravity and extent of our problem.

Recently I had an experience which has begun to make me aware of my own narrow, myopic outlook. I was attending a conference of lay and clergy church leaders from across the United States. It was the most ecumenical conference I had ever attended. Roman Catholics, Orthodox, mainline and evangelical Protestants, charismatics and pentecostals were there. We had gathered because we were concerned about spiritual renewal within our various churches. We had gathered to consider how our churches should respond to the growing secularism in our nation.

As we worshiped, listened to various speakers, and dialogued with one another, something began to happen to me. I began to realize how parochial my understanding of what God is doing in the world had been. Like Peter as he entered the house of Cornelius, who was to become the first Gentile convert, I was being pushed out of my comfortable United Methodist cocoon.

One night during the conference as I lay in bed reflecting upon what was going on, I pictured myself standing inside the gate of the vineyard called United Methodism. This was the vineyard I believed God had called me to labor in—the

93

same vineyard several generations of my family had also labored in as pastors and missionaries. Of course, it was merely one of God's many vineyards. There were Roman Catholic, Presbyterian, and Assemblies of God vineyards along with a host of others. But the United Methodist vineyard was the only one I had ever labored in. I had been born and raised in it. It was all I had ever known. My faith had been nurtured in it. So I loved this vineyard. I would give my life to see it become the fruitful vineyard it once was. For almost twenty years as a pastor in several local churches and as a professor in a theological seminary, I had been laboring in the United Methodist vineyard to that end. Behind me stood the risen Christ. Since he had so many different vineyards, he was not standing inside any one vineyard. He was standing outside the gate of the vineyard, but he was encouraging me and guiding me as I worked for renewal in the vineyard. I was inside trying to represent him and to labor for him. Sometimes during my years of working, as I looked out across the vineyard, I was encouraged as I saw signs of renewal in local congregations and in the denomination. At other times I was discouraged in the face of many indicators of congregational and denominational decline.

So there I was in my mind's eye, standing in the vineyard. The risen Christ was behind me. I was looking out across the vineyard, longing to see it renewed.

And then I did something I had never done before. I turned around, so that instead of looking at the vineyard, I found myself looking at the risen Christ. But instead of facing me as I thought he would be, he was turned around so that he had his back to me. And do you know what he was looking at? He was looking at the world that was out beyond him. That's what he seemed most concerned about—not for the renewal of my vineyard or any of the other vineyards, for that matter, but for the redemption of the world.

Then it struck me that if the redemption of the world is

what he is most concerned about, it ought to be what I am most concerned about too. Obviously, he wants to use all of his vineyards in accomplishing that end. But I realized I had made the renewal of the United Methodist vineyard an end in itself. I was concerned more about that than the purpose of any such renewal: making disciples of all nations.

Then I thought about Methodism's founder, John Wesley. He was concerned about renewing his vineyard—the Church of England. He loved his church and would never separate from it, even though as Methodism grew, many of his followers urged him to separate. But even greater than his love for his church was his love for the world. That was why he disregarded ecclesiastical conventions about parish boundaries. He was more concerned about reaching people in the world for Christ than about maintaining church order—especially when that order kept the church from fulfilling its mission to the world.

Wesley had his feet firmly planted in the vineyard called the Church of England. He couldn't be moved out of it. But he wasn't facing that vineyard. His back was turned toward it. He was facing the risen Christ who in turn was facing the world. And because he was facing the world, not the church, he became a much more effective instrument in renewing the church than if he had been facing the church! Like Wesley, we've got to get beyond the renewal of our vineyard to the redemption of the world. That's what God is most concerned about.

There are scores of faithful United Methodists who are longing to see our church and our local congregations renewed. Like me, they have been laboring in the vineyard to that end. But perhaps like me, they have been so concerned for the renewal of the vineyard that they lack a concern for the redemption of the world. There will not be a renewal of holiness of heart and life among us until there is a renewal in mission. What we need to do is to turn around in the vineyard, quit facing the congregation or the denomination, and face the risen Christ. Join him in his mission to a lost, broken world.

Will United Methodism be renewed or will it continue to decline? I'm convinced now that that is not the most important question. Will we join Christ in his mission in the world?

Like Wesley, we need to look away from ourselves and once again look upon the world as our parish. When we make the world—not our congregations or our denomination—our focus, then it will happen. The people called United Methodist will be renewed. We will be restored as we reach out beyond ourselves to a broken and desperate world.

"Here am I; send me!" It happened to Isaiah. "The world is my parish." It happened to Wesley. May it happen again in United Methodist congregations everywhere! May our passion for holiness drive us to the world for which Christ died.

Notes

1. Albert Outler, *Evangelism in the Wesleyan Spirit* (Nashville: Tidings, 1971), p. 19.
2. *Works*, 1, p. 185.
3. *Works*, 3, p. 479.
4. Quoted in A. Skevington Wood, *The Burning Heart* (Grand Rapids: William B. Eerdmans, Co., 1967), p. 95.
5. *Letters*, I, p. 286.
6. *Works*, 8, p. 310.
7. George Hunter, "Is the World Still Our Parish?" an address given at the Convocation on World Mission and Evangelism, Louisville, Ky., July 10, 1990.
8. The total of 443 overseas missionaries in 1988 combines the number of missionaries of the Board of Global Ministries (416) and the Mission Society for United Methodists (27).